Frontiers of Financial Technology:

Expeditions in future commerce, from blockchain and

digital banking to prediction markets and beyond

Edited by David Shrier and Alex Pentland

www.VisionaryFuture.com

Frontiers of Financial Technology

VISIONARY FUTURE

www.VisionaryFuture.com

Portions of this work were previously published in a white paper series; reproduced with permission of the authors.

EDITED BY:

David Shrier and Alex Pentland

Acknowledgements

To our wives, who gave up several Saturdays and Sundays to allow this book to happen.

CONTENTS

Introduction.. PAGE 1

CHAPTER 1: Blockchain: 5th Horizon of Networked Innovation....................... PAGE 3

CHAPTER 2: Blockchain and Transactions, Markets & Marketplaces............. PAGE 27

CHAPTER 3: Blockchain and Infrastructure (Identity, Data Security) .... PAGE 47

CHAPTER 4: Mobile Money & Payments .... PAGE 67

CHAPTER 5: Prediction Markets .... PAGE 97

CHAPTER 6: Digital Banking Manifesto.. PAGE 117

CHAPTER 7: Policy & Fintech... PAGE 141

CHAPTER 8: Future Directions.. PAGE 205

References .... PAGE 213

Contributor Biographies .... PAGE 231

INTRODUCTION

We didn't set out to write a book.

We began by working on what turned into a series of white papers about leading edge topics as part of our Future Commerce class at MIT. Through conversations with experts on financial technology, data, and identity, at Davos, with the Silicon Valley Executive Network, and within our MIT Future Commerce class, we explored the business, government and academic worlds for the best ways to describe the potential impact of innovations like Blockchain. Matt Reed, Mark Flood, and Oliver Goodenough from the U.S. Treasury's Office of Financial Research proved especially stimulating collaborators for our intellectual journey. In the end, we found that we had distinctive insights to contribute, whether about blockchain's "killer app" or about the ultimate evolution of the digital banking revolution.

While we were writing our whitepaper series, we were preparing our MIT Future Commerce class in fintech entrepreneurship to bridge from on-campus to online. The launch cohort ultimately encompassed 70 countries and over 1,000 students. We realized pretty quickly that there wasn't a good textbook that we could use to introduce students with a general business background to the paradigm shifts roiling the financial services industry.

Hence, the book you now possess.

We recognize that "state of the art" in an emerging field is a moving target, and encourage your feedback.

Now, join us in exploring the frontiers of financial technology.

CHAPTER 1

Blockchain: 5th Horizon of Networked Innovation

David Shrier, Deven Sharma, Alex Pentland

I. INTRODUCTION: THE FIFTH HORIZON OF NETWORKED INNOVATION

How can you capitalize on the disruption that blockchain is introducing into the global financial system? What are the risks and opportunities that this new technology represents? What roles can each of government, academia and private industry play in shaping the new future that blockchain can enable?

While blockchain is, today, an immature technology, it holds the potential to unleash a wave of innovation across multiple industries – including financial services. Just as we saw transformation driven by earlier technologies like the HTTP protocol (unlocking the World Wide Web) and the rise of pervasive computing and intelligent devices (so-called "Internet of Things"), so too blockchain may create new businesses and applications not even dreamed of at this writing.

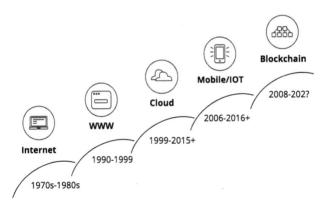

Blockchain: Popular Topic of 2016

Blockchain technology has entered the top strategic priorities of the CEOs of the Fortune 1000[1]. Venture investment in the field has grown to $1 billion in 2015, representing 7% of all Fintech VC funding, with some forecasting investment in blockchain to grow to $10 billion in 2016[2].

Potential for Transformation

Blockchain represents a technology innovation that enables transparent interactions of parties on a new type of trusted and secure network which distributes certified and auditable access to data. Although the technical components have been in existence for decades, blockchain *qua* blockchain is a novel, resilient, and general purpose approach to data, transaction analytics and networks. It holds the potential to address inefficiencies, reduce cost, unlock capital, improve trust in societal fabric, and open new business models. It also could accelerate the growth of the informal economy or even criminal elements of societies, complicating efforts of governments to provide security and safety to their citizens. Like any new technology, it holds the potential for good and for harm, and benefits from an enlightened, informed, and ethical application by its users.

Blockchain has generated extensive interest and enthusiasm in financial markets. Why? Trust and confidence in the promise to meet obligations is the cornerstone of any financial transaction. Substantial parts of financial markets are designed to solve for problems of trust and asymmetry in the financial transactions through the risk management infrastructure.

- Substantial costs in the financial infrastructure are designed for identity checking, transaction authenticating, reliably and accurately transacting, supporting records, and securely storing records. These activities solve for trust, fraud and error.

- Substantial capital and collateral gets locked in the financial system to buffer against lack of trust and confidence in certainty and predictability of outcomes.

- The cost burden of the risk infrastructure makes the economics of small size transactions expensive and unaffordable, and therefore inaccessible to low income members of society.

Blockchain technologies potentially solve for problems in trust, asymmetry of information and economics of small transactions without burdensome risk infrastructure and central intermediaries.

Financial Services Opportunities

In financial services, examples of blockchain applications include the ability to:

- Streamline records transfer of stock ownership;
- Improve speed and reduce cost of syndicated loans, by enabling the possibility of direct syndication;
- Increase transparency into collaterals embedded in many financial transactions;
- Enhance regulatory compliance by automated, instantaneous record validation;
- Reduce costs of money remittance and currency exchange;
- Create self-executing contracts that reduce or eliminate the possibility of fraud or corruption;
- Improve rule of law regarding transfer of property title;
- Eliminate most of the costs and friction in issuance and trading of securities such as equities and debt;
- Reduce cost and improve access in insurance markets by creating the potential for easier implementation of self-insured risk pools;

- Allow the creation of new forms of identity separate from a central issuing authority; and
- Provide a means of exchange of value in systems where trust in central authority has been lost.

Beyond the banking sector of financial services, the impact in the insurance sector will also be substantial from: efficient transaction processing, reduction of claims fraud and better evaluation of risks.

We are seeing blockchain currencies being used to transfer value out of markets where currency regulations are strict and trust in central banks is weak. As this level of activity increases, regulatory authorities will undoubtedly take a more severe view on these activities. Yet, as governments that have attempted to restrict Twitter usage have found, once the genie is out of the bottle, it is difficult to recapture.

New models being pursued range from a primary "distributed trust" structure which makes it possible to use a pseudonymous cryptocurrency like bitcoin that is completely open and public, to permissioned, private, trusted systems, such as those being implemented by some investment firms as a faster, lower-cost means of settling and clearing trades.

A Note of Caution

We are currently in the invention/experimentation state of market evolution with blockchain technology. Today, we can't predict which application will be the "killer app", but the speculation is that as much as $15 billion to $20 billion can be saved in the financial services sector alone using blockchain[4], translating to more than $150 billion of potential equity value creation based on current market multiples. These savings will primarily come through greater efficiency, i.e., job loss. Benefits from unlocking collateral and greater liquidity might be substantial as well.

Barriers to Adoption

Many hurdles remain towards adopting this new technology, and as with any new tool, human and organization attitude poses a high barrier, including:

- **Standards:** An absence of well-adopted standards in documentation and practices exists, for example, even invoice and bill formats are unique to each issuing organization although varying formats adds very limited value. Standards could start with industry specific action, or be government initiated;
- **Organization and Human Behavior:** Behavior to embrace and adopt harmonized standards and practices is difficult to achieve;
- **Infrastructure legacy:** Given large existing infrastructure within any organization, the costs of replacing existing technology with new Blockchain investment are high;
- **Confidentiality:** Protection of private and confidential information and comprising competitive advantage;
- **Processing cost:** High and escalating cost of proof verification;
- **Legal and regulation:**
    - Settlement finality and dispute resolution – consumer risk protection;
    - Liability of security risk and related losses driven by introducing a new financial infrastructure;
    - Protection against risk of attack or dominance by few players – may discourage players to link "off-chain" assets – as well as anti-trust regulations and implications;
    - Conduct: priority of verification of transactions;
    - Regulation and legal classification jurisdictions of assets, data location & flow and how existing regulations apply.

Looming Dislocations

The rise of digital media in the 1980s led to a disruption of the newspaper industry, ultimately reshaping the face of media globally. Copyeditors, press operators, delivery agents, even paid journalists, all became redundant in an era of Huffington Post and Twitter. We see the potential for similar levels of disruption in the financial services, supply chain and logistics, and other industries. One startup recently formed at MIT by students in our Future Commerce class on Fintech innovation suggests removing three to five layers of intermediation between poor farmers and global agribusiness suppliers. This represents benefit to the farmer, and to the supplier, but could ultimately result in the loss of 5 to 25 jobs among the intermediaries for that single transaction stream.

Efforts to convince people to adopt blockchain technology could result in the pursuit of "Potemkin village" solutions, without tangible benefit, or with benefits that generate perverse outcomes (such as the creation of additional cost). There are examples in other industries of failed promise of technology. For example, electronic medical records (EMRs) were hailed as a revolution in medicine that would transform health outcomes, but a 2009 study by the European Commission spanning 10 countries showed the benefits to primarily be financial in nature[5]. Validating this, the Chief Medical Officer of a top-3 EMR company shared with the authors that EMRs were optimized for financial reporting, not clinical care, and were never intended to improve health outcomes – in no small part because the "buyer" of the technology was the chief financial officer of the provider organization. This has created market opportunity for more user-friendly EMRs, but the most widely-adopted EMRs are built around billing improvement not medical care quality. One could argue that this has contributed to the continued rise of healthcare costs in the U.S., to 17% of GDP in 2015[6].

Given the potential as well as the dangers of blockchain development, we ask:

- How can policy interventions shape the future of blockchain in productive directions?
- Is there any way to effectively manage productivity improvements, that may lead to significant employment disruption in financial services?
- What steps can we take to mitigate the negative impacts of innovation-driven employment dislocation?

To answer these questions, we need to understand the evolution of blockchain and draw parallels to similar technology (re/e)volutions.

An Origin Story

The antecedents of the current environment have been developing for some time, since the publication of the bitcoin protocol in October 2008. We note that the first blockchain applications emerged out of eroded trust in traditional institutions, yet eight years later, more than 60% of the global financial system has entered into a consortium to apply blockchain to remove cost and create efficiency in their businesses. Have we gone from "revolution now!" to "reengineering processes"?

In the summer of 2014, MIT hosted the Ecology of Digital Assets summit, leading to the creation and adoption of the Windhover Principles[7] for anti-money-laundering (AML) and Know Your Customer (KYC) compliance among over 20 bitcoin and blockchain companies in informal consultation with U.S. government officials. At MIT, we have developed new open-source technology solutions such as Enigma[8] for secure data management and CoreID[9] to address some of the issues related to AML/KYC in cryptocurrencies, but are only beginning to see awareness of the need, much less moves for adoption. Understanding and adoption of compliance solutions remains weak both within the fintech startup community and among regulatory agencies.

In our conversation with global leaders at Davos this past January 2016, we heard rising interest in the C-suite around blockchain technologies as a tool for transformation in the financial services industry. The theme has continued in 2016 as we see top tier financial institutions funding both external experimentation and setting up internal "skunk works" groups to develop blockchain applications. Governments, as well, have begun to explore how blockchain can address certain intractable issues of trust and transparency. Yet, the technology, commercial models and adoption, and the regulatory and legal frameworks surrounding blockchain, remain in their infancy.

According to the World Economic Forum's survey on technology tipping points, 58% of respondents expect that by the year 2025, 10% of global GDP will be stored on blockchain variations, up from about 0.008% in March 2016.

The Evolution of a New Technology

We are in the early stages ("invention/experimentation") of the adoption of blockchain. As with other new technologies, blockchain is undergoing a phase of invention and experimentation. Blockchain is a revolutionary innovation in its approach to building trust, transparency and traceability in financial transactions. The innovation is in the **concept and approach** of piecing together **technology components**, not necessarily a technology magic silver bullet.

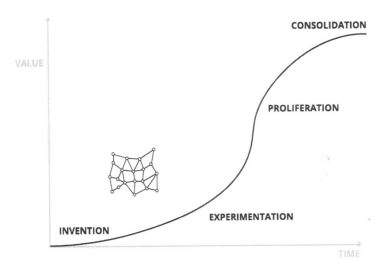

Just as ARPANET led to the Internet and ultimately the World Wide Web, we have early precursors like SETI@HOME and Amazon Mechanical Turk leading to the rise of distributed networks and outsourced distributed computations and tasks. Despite the high degree of excitement, a large number of venture capital investments in the sector are funding a proliferation of companies built on immature technology.

If we examine the evolution of networked innovation, the 1970s and 1980s saw the development of the Internet, the "first horizon" in our paradigm. Beginning in 1990, Sir Tim Berners-Lee and others promoted the creation of intuitive navigation and cross-connection of information, making possible the "second horizon" of the World Wide Web. While "cloud computing" had its origins in other technologies, we argue that the formation of Salesforce.com in 1999 marked a key milestone in its evolution into the "third horizon" of networked innovation[10]. A notable publication around Byzantine Fault Tolerance (critical to the theoretical underpinnings of blockchain), and the launch of projects like SETI@

Home (which anticipates the distributed nodes of blockchain), also were produced in 1999. With decreasing bandwidth costs and increasing ubiquity of smart phones and smart devices, we trace the "fourth horizon" to the launch of mobile broadband services in 2006. This brings us to the blockchain, with Satoshi's October 2008 paper launching the "fifth horizon".

The current state of blockchain industry reminds the authors of the early days of World Wide Web commercialization, as chronicled in Michael Wolff's Burn Rate. While a large number of companies are being funded, not all with sound business models, some hold the potential to become the next Google, the next Apple, or the next Facebook.

In 1993, no one could have realistically envisioned an Uber, or an Airbnb, or a viable ZipCar. In 2001, no one could have predicted Facebook's success (an earlier version of a "university-member-driven-social-network", The Square, was a casualty of the dotcom bust) or YouTube's market dominance (bandwidth constraints and other issues led companies like Broadcast.com and TheFeedroom to relatively modest outcomes). And today, in 2016, we can only dimly imagine what the "killer app" for blockchain will be. The near-term future is somewhat more clear, and we will concentrate the majority of our discussion on the 5-year horizon of blockchain innovation and financial services.

A Call to Action

In our discussions with an array of individuals among industry, academia, and policymakers, the authors have found that understanding of blockchain is poor, and appreciation is modest of both the dangers that the technology can generate as well as the benefits it can deliver. We observe a generalized awareness, but heterogeneous comprehension of the nuances.

Recognizing the need for strategic clarity, and framework solutions, the Massachusetts Institute of Technology's Connection Science & Engineering team seeks to offer context on the blockchain revolution, pose policy questions to regulators and lawmakers, and provide inspiration to blockchain innovators.

MIT is frequently called a place where "the future is invented," informed by our mission of solving humanity's biggest problems. Our belief institutionally is that innovation can be a positive force for change, if guided by a responsible, ethical framework. Despite the notes of caution that we inject into this report, we believe that blockchain technology can deliver material benefits to society, and will provide guidance around potential areas for application that we feel hold promise.

We invite you to enter the fifth horizon of innovation, and help us create the future of blockchain.

II. HOW BLOCKCHAIN WORKS

Blockchain and its Attributes

Blockchain is a distributed database with an open ledger. Broadly, this means data isn't stored on a single computer but rather on many different computers (known as "nodes") in a peer-to-peer network. This represents a radical paradigm shift in financial services. Blockchain's democratization principles has captured the imagination of the financial market place:

- Distributed data ledgers used, updated and verified by participants in the blockchain versus centralized data base
- Identity verification and authentication executed by the participants
- Logic and rules embedded in the transaction versus in a separate application layer
- Traceability of changes from the beginning
- Documents maintained separate from the ledgers

Centralized Ledgers

Traditional centralized ledger systems, such as those used by central banks to manage sovereign currencies, have one central ledger, which records currency transactions. Trust is centralized within a single entity who is tasked with governing the management of sales, purchases and transfers of the currency. Centralized ledgers have the advantages of organizational simplicity, control through a single point

CENTRALIZED

of record-keeping, and lower cost to maintain. Disadvantages include limitations on scalability, the potential for hacking and other security concerns, and the risk that if the central authority either shuts down or decides to unilaterally alter the record, there's nothing the individual can do about it (short of legal recourse).

Decentralized Ledgers

In a decentralized ledger, there are multiple copies of the ledger stating who owns what. I go to my money transfer agent, to whom I hand cash. My agent records that in their system. He contacts another broker in a foreign country who exchanges my dollars for their pesos or euros, and records the transaction in their system. Later the two agents meet up to reconcile accounts. There are multiple copies of the

DECENTRALIZED

ledger, but they are brought into agreement through trusted parties. This system has some benefits of redundancy, but still places control into a few hands and has reconciliation challenges.

Distributed Ledgers

With a distributed ledger, each node has a copy of the ledger. A consensus voting system, where more than 50% of nodes need to agree on a transaction to effectuate it, makes properly-designed networks of nodes exceedingly difficult to hack.

DISTRIBUTED

The advantages of distributed ledgers over other systems are:

* Resiliency

* Security

* Creation of trust

The reason blockchain is called a "chain" is that there is an initial block, called a genesis block, to start the chain. When you want to perform a transaction, such as to sell a bitcoin or another cryptocurrency to another person:

- The blockchain software puts out a call for the nodes in the distributed network to perform a calculation to create a "hash", or encoding of the transaction details, allowing for later verification.

- The act of choosing a random number, whose hash results in the desired value with respect to a target chain value, is referred to as "mining".

- The new block links back to the previous block, in this case the genesis block, creating a "chain". As each new block is mined, the chain lengthens.

- The calculation conducted presents what is known as "proof of work". This serves to validate adding blocks to the chain, and allows for defense against bad actors by having the entire network create the system of trust, versus needing to trust each party (or node) on the network.

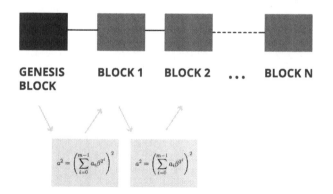

Let's look at how the bitcoin blockchain works (from the Economist):

> Every ten minutes or so mining computers collect a few hundred pending bitcoin transactions (a "block") and turn them into a mathematical puzzle. The first miner to find the solution announces it to others on the network. The other miners then check whether the sender of the funds has the right to spend the money, and whether the solution to the puzzle is correct. If enough of them grant their approval, the block is cryptographically added to the ledger and the miners move on to the next set of transactions (hence the term "blockchain"). The miner who found the solution gets 25 bitcoins as a reward, but only after another 99 blocks have been added to the ledger. All this gives miners an incentive to participate in the system and validate transactions. Forcing miners to solve puzzles in order to add to the ledger provides protection: to double-spend a bitcoin, digital bank-robbers would need to rewrite the blockchain, and to do that they would have to control more than half of the network's puzzle-solving capacity[11].

Interestingly enough, although "proof of work", used to be central to blockchain theory, it has (at least in the case of bitcoin) become a bit of a burden. Some industry executives believe that the bitcoin blockchain spends $600 million per year on proof of work most of which is currently carried out by three bitcoin server farms in Asia[12].

Blockchain isn't a panacea. Artificial limits built into the bitcoin experiment mean that it will never be a widely used currency despite the fact that as of August 2016 it is valued at approximately $9 billion. Other forms of blockchain may enjoy wider adoption. Moreover, many early users of the bitcoin blockchain were engaged in illicit commerce and were seeking to avoid government scrutiny. (The authors note that other fringe markets have developed and adopted new technology before they became mainstream, like streaming video or micropayments).

Consolidation in the mining of bitcoin, which has become computationally (and thus energy-wise) expensive, has placed significant mining capacity into a few hands, which introduces the risk of defrauding the network – defeating the original purpose of the distributed network. This may promote adoption of new cryptocurrencies, but may also weaken trust in the paradigm for consumer and corporate adoption of digital currency.

The bitcoin blockchain's scalability is currently hindered by a 1MB limit on the amount of data allowed in each block, which at some point will curtail the number of transactions that can be confirmed in any 10-minute period. Bitcoin developers have been unable to reach consensus on how to change the protocol to address this problem, with one side fearing that larger blocks will require miners to maintain more data storage, which could further favor a more centralized, industrial market structure for mining. Pieter Wuille from Blockstream has proposed a method called "segregated witness" to reduce the amount of data required for each transaction so as to allow more to be included in a block. Others, including Joseph Poon and Thaddeus Dryjas of the Lightning Network, have suggested methods for processing transactions "off chain" before aggregating their data into a single entry in a bitcoin block. It's not clear that either solution will be effective or sufficient to permit a continued expansion in the rate of bitcoin transactions.

Other forms of blockchain are enjoying growing adoption, such as Ethereum, which has created a platform for smart contracts. Unlike the Bitcoin blockchain, which requires substantial expertise to learn how to program, developers can begin building applications on Ethereum using the Solidity programming language in a matter of days or weeks. Industry incumbents have begun supporting Ethereum, such as Microsoft, which added support for Ethereum applications to Visual Studio in collaboration with ConsenSys in March 2016. As with bitcoin, however, there have been problems with the Ethereum system.

An Ideological-Technological Exploration of Blockchain

Most blockchain taxonomies focus on the functional architecture (is it permissioned or permissionless? Is it public or private?). We find useful the division proposed by ArthurB (https://medium. com/@arthurb/a-functional-nomenclature-of-cryptographic-ledgers-e836cb0e6864#.4e3pr7g4u), although it has been pointed out that his statement "Applications which do not attempt to evade oppressive governments have little or no reasons to use decentralized systems" isn't precisely true. There are numerous examples of a need for trust technologies when absolute trust in a third party is absent, having nothing to do with governments – eBay selling is the most trivial example, but equities security trading would be another.

In our view, understanding implementation of blockchain requires understanding implementers, users, and their respective objectives. This context-based analysis of blockchain provides a novel lens on selecting a platform and allocating resources to it. Broadly speaking, when we incorporate ideology into the technological analysis, we see three broad categories:

- **Libertarians:** A substantial number of bitcoiners believe that government has no role in regulating society, and bitcoin usage is an expression of political belief. AML/KYC is anathema to their belief systems. This isn't to say that all bitcoin users and companies feel this way – to the contrary, a large number of bitcoin companies employ or developed policies based on the Windhover Principles that MIT helped shepherd. Rather, a vocal segment of bitcoin miners and developers assert a proprietary ownership of the technology, and vigorously reject anything that compromises their idealized view of how it should be used. To quote a recent post on Reddit: "if you aren't working to make Bitcoin better (read: more private, more fungible, more scalable) then you should keep your dirty, groveling sycophant paws off of it."[13] It's a vigorously-expressed point of view but one shared by a number of users who engage each other regularly in self-reinforcement.

- **Technocrats:** A broad middle of technocrats don't automatically assume either government regulation or total freedom from regulation, but rather see blockchain as a flexible technology without ideology. Ethereum would fall clearly into this category.

- **Rules Followers:** The industry-led consortia such as R3 and Hyperledger accept, *a priori,* that regulation applies to blockchain, particularly with respect to AML/KYC as it applies to currency and other financial-related matters. While perhaps not as passionate in espousing their views as the Libertarians, these Rules Followers are making an ideological choice embedded into the fabric of their chosen technology platform. (Corda doesn't technically use "blocks" but we are describing all distributed ledger technologies as blockchain for convenience)[14].

Longer-term use of blockchain at scale will likely come from Technocrats or Rules Followers. At same time, the passion that the libertarians feel has caused them to think "outside the box" and question assumptions, resulting in a new way of transacting that is transparent, open and decentralized. In fact, blockchain as such would not exist with those passionate libertarians driving its creation and adoption.

Let a Thousand Blockchains Bloom

With the proliferation of funding for blockchain has come a proliferation of blockchains. And, with this, comes the need for interoperability. Enter the InterLedger Protocol, which seeks to interlink the companies, individuals and technologies behind this proliferation[15]. Facing the proliferation of blockchains, Ripple and others in the industry are seeking to provide a better mechanism for connecting blockchains to each other, while preserving the security of private blockchains. The Hyperledger Project, likewise, seeks to disseminate an open standard for distributed ledgers to facilitate connectivity.

How will the path to adoption broaden?

The extraordinary promise of blockchain initiates a conversation and likely leads to experimentation. The development of foundational blocks would accelerate the path of adoption. Tools that support the activity flow might accelerate the adoption.

What is the Likely Path to Adoption?

There are several possible paths for adoption of blockchain, which are not mutually exclusive but might potentially become mutually reinforcing over time. We see three primary axes of adoption:

- **Incumbent Intra-Organization Permissioned/Private Blockchain:** Most organizations operate with enormous silos that lead to friction in information sharing and duplicating of work. Adoption of Blockchains within an organization might raise the openness and comfort in adopting across organizations/external parties.

- **Incumbent Inter-Organization Permissioned/Private Blockchain:** A plausible scenario is where organizations apply the concepts underlying blockchain to their existing technology infrastructure, and gradually migrate to new technologies over time.

- **New Ventures:** Many new ventures have already been funded that are experimenting at all levels of the technology stack. These new ventures explore both foundational components (the ledger, smart contracts, other kinds of smart assets) and experimentation into challenge areas (e.g., provenance for diamonds; property rights in countries with weak rule of law; remittance of funds across borders or currencies).

What mechanisms can be put into place to facilitate adoption and continued innovation? How can governments, private citizens, companies and academia best collaborate to empower this exploration and growth?

III. TOWARDS THE FIFTH HORIZON OF NETWORKED INNOVATION

How can we proceed towards development of this fifth horizon of networked innovation? The issues of blockchain are as much about technology and business model development as it is about regulation and industry dynamics. 2015 was about gaining attention for the technology. 2016 will be about rapid and widespread experimentation with this new technology.

Joichi Ito, Director of the MIT Media Lab, wrote this note of caution: "Many people are so excited about the potential applications [of blockchain] that they have ignored completely the architecture of the system on which they would run. Just as many Internet companies assume that the Internet works on its own, they assume that all blockchains are the same and work, but blockchain technology is not as mature as the Internet where you can almost get away with that... Governments and banks are launching all kind of plans without enough thought going into how they're actually going to build the secure ledger."

In strategic discussions with regulators, the authors were invited to contemplate not only the positive potential of blockchain, but also the dystopian inverse, where the promise of blockchain failed to materialize. Imagine a world where five of the largest banks collapse due to coding errors that result in hundreds of thousands of smart contracts mis-executing. It's possible: in 2012, Knight Trading collapsed due to a $460 million trading error; shifting the decimal a few places to the right could have a systemic impact on the global financial system. What if quantum computing breakthroughs were combined with blockchain to create a truly impenetrable money-laundering network for criminals? Perhaps scariest of all for the investors who have poured billions into blockchain: what if, 10 years from now, there is no meaningful adoption of blockchain?

Another issue that the bitcoin blockchain community will need to confront first, but that is faced by all mining-incentive-driven markets, is that the security of the chain can disappear if mining becomes unprofitable.

The authors remain convinced that the potential benefits outweigh the possible downside scenarios. New avenues of exploration may expose previously unconsidered opportunity. Imagine a world where the internet of distributed autonomous devices meets the internet of distributed data. What if the smart cars driving on the roads in a city and the smart buildings around which they drove were linked in a network that powered the financial system of the country? What if idle capacity of autonomous vehicles were harnessed to oversee efficient distribution of goods and services? It could be wonderful, or it could be a nightmare.

Such difficult problems may end up stimulating widespread adoption of blockchain technology. We believe that cybersecurity, and specifically data security, may be one such application. A blockchain-based system such as Enigma[16] represents a means of storing critically sensitive corporate data in a virtually hack-proof decentralized network, yet still perform computation on the data while it remains encrypted. We are also intrigued with the notion of "bringing the algorithm to the data", rather than the current model of separation of data from computation.

Yet, adoption is an open question. Is there an incentive structure that could be derived that would encourage a notoriously siloed, and competitive, industry like financial services to form a community with free flow of ideas to adopt uniform standards? How could this be developed and promoted?

CHAPTER 2

Blockchain and Transactions, Markets & Marketplaces

David Shrier, Jaclyn Iarossi,
Deven Sharma, Alex Pentland

I. INTRODUCTION: TRANSACTIONS, MARKETS & MARKETPLACES

In our previous chapter, we provided a framework describing blockchain as a "fifth horizon of networked innovation", and outlined basic principles of how the technology operates (both in a technical sense and in a socio-political context). In this chapter, we will look at the future impact of blockchain on transactions, markets and marketplaces.

Blockchain technology has the potential to address a number of sectors. We will focus our discussion on:

- **Securities trading:** potential to exceed US$20 billion in cost savings among incumbent financial companies, and possibly drive significant disruption within the existing financial ecosystem.

- **Commercial & Retail Banking:** accessing the US$ 2 trillion credit gap globally.

- **Insurance:** addressing the US$40 billion uninsured in the "protection gap".

Exploiting these opportunities will have profound implications for the numerous intermediaries currently serving these sectors.

Many facets of today's markets and marketplaces are likely to be impacted by large-scale adoption of blockchain technology, creating many new avenues for value creation. Focusing on a few key applications areas for institutional players and Small to Medium-sized Enterprises (SMEs), impact from blockchain technology can range from increasing global access to finance, creating new transaction types and reimagining existing exchange and structural models.

Most transactions are accompanied with data that give them intelligence. For example, data underlying transactions may include information to complete a transaction such as the account and routing number of the payor and payee that identify the source, and receiver and all intermediaries through which the transaction may have passed. Increasingly, transactions also include additional information attributes on participant location and behavior. Data associated with each transaction provides critical information on transaction instruments and the risks associated.

A transaction, such as a typical non-cash payment, can be distilled into elements: Originator, Funding, Instrument, Usage, Processing, Receiver, Confirmation and Settlement. The data attached to transactions raises a fundamental tension: ample data aids in protecting fraud risk, creates opportunity to offer or receive more personalized service, but increases privacy risk. A payment trail, defined as the intermediaries involved and who thus have access to the data on the transaction, also adds to the risk. Cash has no intermediary. Early forms of electronic payment with credit card have six intermediaries: Payor, Website/App Operator, Merchant/Payee, Merchant Bank (Acquirer), Card Network, Customer/Payor Issuer. Different intermediaries have varying practices of capturing, retaining and using the data and as such, the longer the trail the greater the risk.

Fundamentally, advantages that blockchain offers include:

- **Security:** consensus resolution of ledger entries creates a more resilient and robust security framework

- **Shared ledger:** greater auditability and transparency provides greater trust. Absence of a central intermediary can make micropayments more economical

- **Encryption:** the enhanced security afforded by blockchain provides for more confidence to conduct larger value and riskier transactions

- **Embedding application logic within a transaction:** one can use data attributes embedded in the transaction to make transaction flow conditional on time, location, event, trust level, etc., which creates pathways for automated interactions, eliminating cost and improving speed via vehicles such as smart contracts

Blockchain provides the capability to collapse the transaction trail, and still offer traceability and transparency. Not only can it speed up the process, but also reduce the risk associated with the completion of the transaction and misuse of any data.

II. COMMERCIAL & RETAIL BANKING

While approximately 95% of the world's businesses are SMEs, as many as half of them cannot get the financing they need – a credit gap estimated at over $2 trillion across over 200 million businesses[2].

A. Collateral Registries

Often a lack of sufficient collateral serves as a limiting factor on the ability of SMEs to secure a loan, particularly in developing countries. According to the World Bank globally almost 80% of all enterprise loans require collateral, which on average needs to be valued at 202.7% of the loan amount.[3]

While property is internationally accepted as a form of collateral, moveable assets such as receivables or inventory frequently are not, and yet comprise the majority of SME value. Wider use of movable assets as collateral is limited by a lack of trusted, central collateral registries which currently require government support and funding.

How impactful is a trusted movable assets registry? In a 2013 study of over a 100 countries, those that implemented collateral registry reform saw an 8% increase in access to credit for SMEs.[4] Further work by the IMF saw significant increases to access to credit and lower costs of credit. "In countries where security interests are perfected and there is a predictable priority system for creditors in case of default, credit to GDP averages 60 percent, compared with 30 percent to 32 percent of average for countries without a clear creditor protection system. In industrial countries, borrowers using collateral get nine times the level of credit, repayment periods up to eleven times longer, and interest rates 50 percent lower than borrowers without collateral." Systemically, it also reduces financial institutional risk by increasing diversification of assets, offering opportunities to lenders to increase market share and short-term liquidity of those assets.[5]

Despite overwhelmingly positive benefits many countries have yet to implement collateral registries and inconsistent standards exist globally. Blockchain technology means that creation of these registries will no longer depend on government sponsorship. Using best practices already established by international agencies such as the IMF, SMEs could register their assets and grant access to potential lenders offering better information to make credit decisions.

An added benefit for SMEs to register their goods: fraud reduction. According to Sylvain Theveniaud, managing director of Allianz Accelerator "a definitive registry to trace ownership and certify provenance of big-ticket items would root out illegal goods and decrease fraud worldwide."[6] The value of blockchain is significant in potentially mitigating the $1.77 trillion cross-border counterfeit goods market.[7]

B. Smart Property

In September 2014, China and Hong Kong had amassed a $13.5 billion commodity trade discrepancy in just 9 months. It is believed that to circumvent Chinese capital import laws, fake commodity invoices were created leading to manipulation of export numbers as well as the yuan.[8] If the trades represented by these disputed invoices were required to share one ledger there would be no way to arrive at any settlement differences.

The diamond industry derives a lot of its value based on provenance. To combat blood diamonds and prove the value of the stone there is an industry-wide initiative to implement Everledger, a distributed platform that creates a unique digital fingerprint for each diamond so it can be tracked through all borrowers straight to its origin.[9]

But what if we could move one step further in validating underlying collateral or commodities are where and what was promised? Combining blockchain with another growing technological force, the Internet of

Things, could unleash a powerful new idea, smart property. If a physical asset was embedded with sensors, the property would record any transaction where ownership changed hands or alert parties that terms of a contract may not be satisfied. Using oil as an example, before agreeing to the terms of a deal, the exact chemical composition and weight of a barrel of oil would be known. If a storm disrupted shipping times, a cargo ship could trigger contingency clauses of a contract and alert impacted parties.

Collateral management could be even more streamlined. If a business puts its inventory up as collateral, the collateral value could dynamically update improving the risk and collateral management teams supporting the loan more like a securities-backed loan. For any type of collateral utilizing a collateral ledger and smart contracts, the parties could agree upfront on specific reference data, be it information within the company or external macro data, automatically triggering and either satisfy or alert all parties to a collateral call. Closing the gap on collateral management could have a huge net effect, inefficiencies in the global collateral management market are estimated to cost banks up to $4 billion annually.[10]

C. Commercial Payments / New SME Opportunities

There has been a question around blockchain technology of what is the real use case? Is this just a solution in search of a problem? Micropayments are an example of a problem-space suitable for a peer-to-peer low cost value transfer method. Poised to help redefine many business models, micropayments are transactions less than $10. The idea of online micropayments were championed by IBM and Netscape so much so that they lobbied the World Wide Web Consortium (W3C) to develop universal micropayment standards - there is even an error code 402 built into the web for Payment Required[11, 12].

Micropayments never gained critical mass before as they were not financially feasible and many businesses saw no need for revenue streams beyond advertising and subscriptions. The normal business model of taking a small percentage of each transaction is prohibitively expensive for high volume low value payments.[13] The exorbitant expense comes from transmitting the data associated with transaction and processing to complete the transaction. The world of ecommerce looks very different now, with diminishing advertising margins and subscription models still proving difficult.

Other SME micropayment opportunities are additionally emerging. Gyft provides gift cards to SMEs who previously were not large enough to support the necessary payment infrastructure, a nice boon since 65% of consumers spend 38% more than the face value of their gift cards according to CEB. Gyft ultimately wants to fundamentally change gift cards by creating a standardized trading platform for gift cards and see their issuance through blockchain to reduce issuance costs. Consumers could easily exchange gift cards and never lose the card value.[14]

III. SECURITIES & TRADING

Trade and collateral finance are one of many financial spaces that startups and incumbent players are creating new solutions underpinned by blockchain technology. Ideas covering commercial payments, capital markets and beyond are all receiving attention and funding.

A. Capital Markets / Institutional Changes

Today's capital markets infrastructure, systems, processes and regulation are overly complex and built when the financial world looked very different from today. Looking through the entire lifecycle of a trade, there are a number of significant areas that in an ideal state, is implemented as the underlying infrastructure, shown in this exhibit[15]:

PRE-TRADE	TRADE	POST-TRADE	CUSTODY & SECURITIES SERVICING
• Transparency and verification of holdings	• Secure, real-time transaction matching, and immediate irrevocable settlement	• No central clearing for real-time cash transactions	• Primary issuance directly onto a blockchain
• Reduced Credit exposures	• Automatic DVP on a cash ledger	• Reduced margin/collateral requirements	• Automation and de-duplication of servicing processes
• Mutualisation of static data	• Automatic reporting & more transparent supervision for market authorities	• Faster novation and efficient post-trade processing	• Richer central datasets with flat accounting hierarchies
• Simpler KYC/KYCC[1] via look through to holding	• Higher AML[2] standards	• Fungible use of assets on blockchains as collateral	• Common reference data
		• Auto-execution of smart contracts	• Fund subscriptions/ redemptions processed automatically on the blockchain
			• Simplification of fund, servicing, accouting, allocations and administration

[1]KYC - Know your Customer, KYCC - Know your Customer's Customer
[2]AML - Anti-money Laundering

Some of the areas with the greatest promise for improvement over the current state include asset ownership, new financial instruments and settlement.

B. Asset Issuance and ownership

Assets could be issued directly into the blockchain ledger. When transactions take place to buy or sell it would simply involve entries being matched in a peer to peer method, with clear ownership based on identify or in the case of a broker someone with clear permission acting on someone else's behalf. This collapses many layers of intermediaries and complexity required under the current system.

For example, shares would be issued digitally via the blockchain and tied to the owners' and/or brokers' identity not an intermediary or custodian as they are today. This is a powerful change for several reasons, because the settlement of cash and the securities exchange could be simultaneous. Faster settlement and elimination of paper certificates would reduce costs. Most importantly share owners would be able to ensure all the rights granted by ownership, which are not always guaranteed by today's system. Today as a cost reduction initiative almost all shares are technically owned by a subsidiary of the Depository Trust & Clearing Corporation (DTCC), so that paper stock transfers are kept in one place and accounted for by one entity.

As recent as a 2015 ruling on the Dell acquisition some shareholders lost their appraisal rights in Delaware court simply because shares had to be retitled in order for the physical paper to be stored without an additional fee, meaning that there was not continuous ownership.[16] While there are several compounding factors in this case, the issue here is that there are broader issues with the system which could be addressed with a digital, secure asset. Going even further would to have all shareholder votes recorded directly on the asset, which means the entire voting history of that share could be attached to the share, regardless of ownership change.

Several companies have started playing with this type of asset issuance today. The most prominent took place in December 2015. Created by a partnership between Nasdaq and Chain, the Linq platform issued and settled the first securities transaction using blockchain backed technology. This was a private equity issuance to a US investor for a private amount.[17]

C. Settlement & Reconciliation

As shown with the collateral trade differences, having only one version of the truth is extremely beneficial to a settlement and reconciliation process. With reducing the number of parties required to execute one transaction and working off a shared ledger has the ability to greatly reduce reconciliation process both with external parties and for internal systems. Distributed ledger technology is projected to reduce costs associated with cross-border payments, securities trading and regulatory compliance by $15-20 billion per year by 2022.[18]

What does this mean in practice for post-trade settlement? First ownership transfer and payment could be simultaneous, cutting counterparty risk down from T+3 to minutes, or whatever timeframe is deemed ideal for the security type. Counterparty risk is further decreased with significant reduction in asymmetric information through counterparty transaction history, immediate collateral information updates, full asset title records and more. Implementing robust smart contracts means that parts of deals could be settled machine to machine rather than requiring significant manual confirms. Lastly, monitoring parties, regulatory or agreed third-party, could be granted access to have complete transaction details and be able to real-time monitor.

Yet, at the same time, instantaneous settlement (or even settlement in a few minutes) will eliminate some of the flexibility inherent in the current system. For example, T+3 allows for borrowing against and lending of shares purely as a broker-based transaction, allowing greater speculation capabilities on the part of rapid traders – something that will be lost in a world with no float. Should a market be constructed only for long-term holders, or should it also facilitate high frequency traders and short-term speculators? Do those short-term players provide for greater liquidity and price flexibility in a dynamic market environment?

Execution errors are another issue that blockchain complicates. The BATS exchange had to withdraw its 2012 IPO due to a programming error, requiring a 4-year wait until it could finally go public in 2016. While current settlement systems allow for a voiding and reconciliation process, imagine the challenges of "rollback" in a blockchain world: by definition, blockchain is an irrevocable record. Furthermore, an automated series of "irrevocable" trades using blockchain could create a cascading series of errors that become difficult to unwind – without the simplicity of a database rollback, the dependent nature of the "chain" creates a new kind of complexity on resolving errors. The so-called "Lehman Hairball" (of interdependent derivatives contracts) still hasn't been resolved six years later. If not proactively designed, a blockchain-based market might be even more opaque.

D. Financial Instruments and Smart Contracts

With more information (i.e. decreased asymmetric information), property and digital IP more publically available new niche derivatives will become possible as underlying assets are more transparent and secondary markets significantly easier to create. Going a step further, needs of company could be broken down to individual cash flows, then bundled to create all new swaps.

The biggest boom to financial engineering comes in the form of Smart Contracts – computer programmable contracts that are verified and enforced electronically. Chris DeRose, community director of the Counterparty Foundation believes that smart contracts create risk reduction through non-discriminatory execution.[19] It creates a cheap, previously agreed method to ensure that all parts of a contract are fulfilled without interference.

IV. INSURANCE

The global insurance industry is acutely aware of the "insurance protection gap" – the idea that there are a large number of people who should have insurance but don't. According to industry trade group The Geneva Association, the emerging markets comprise 40% of the world's GDP but only 17% of its insured population. Globally, 4 billion people are uninsured, representing notional premiums of US$40 billion annually[20].

Blockchain-based smart contracts could provide for automated claims handling and processing, making for a cost-effective microinsurance solution. When combined with other solutions, such as machine learning systems and pattern recognition technology, one could imagine a property & casualty world in which auto claims, for example, could be assessed via an automated system analyzing images captured via a mobile phone, and a claim could be adjudicated in a matter of minutes instead of days or weeks.

An even more disruptive application of blockchain is in the area of peer-to-peer insurance, circumventing established companies (if the regulatory issues are addressed). For example, Uber or Lyft drivers, who currently rely mainly on their personal auto policies, could pool their money on a blockchain and create a smart contract to insure each other, DeRose says. "That's what insurance companies do now, only they govern the pool and take money off the top," he says. "If you have an unbreakable chain of identity to issue an insurance policy, why do you need an insurance company at all?"[21]

As with other intermediated markets, new technology such as distributed cryptographic ledgers could reduce cost and improve access in insurance.

V. PRIVACY

We will get into greater detail on questions of privacy in our next chapter about Infrastructure. However, it is worth noting that transparency on transactions may have the unintended consequence of revealing proprietary trading strategies that financial investors have developed – making it less attractive for them to participate in a market. How can privacy of individuals and firms be appropriately managed in a system that is fundamentally designed for transparency? Zero-knowledge proofs[22] may be a partial answer, where critical or relevant information can be queried (such as: does this entity have enough funds to cover the margin call?) without revealing other data (such as: what is this entity's total portfolio value?).

VI. RETHINKING INTERMEDIARIES AND OTHER MARKET PARTICIPANTS

One of the biggest systemic questions for the mass implementation of blockchain in financial markets centers on the role of counterparties and intermediaries. The current system of intermediation arose out of needs to manage risk, particularly when securities were transacted using paper instruments. While intermediaries have adapted somewhat to digital environments, they have no incentives to reduce margin or eliminate their roles entirely.

When envisioning the future state for capital markets, it is important to remember that technology introduction has previously created opportunity to reduce the number of intermediaries. Computing technology, and later the internet, helped lead to disintermediation and ultimately the creation of the DTCC. This paradigm shift created efficiency savings as well as reducing risk for a system too complex for the new technical realities of finance.

A significant market benefit of blockchain is the collapsing of additional custodial layers, achievable through use of a single ledger and transparent audit. Retrofitting the technology to current processes will inevitably limit how far forward capital markets can be developed, and how many layers of intermediation can be removed. Rethinking the entire transaction system would allow for more profound efficiencies to be introduced, but also creates transition risk.

So what do the future intermediaries look like? Focusing on the core functions that intermediaries play today, there are several roles that will need to be considered.

While who or what performs these functions may differ on based on the asset class, these functions are still required for a properly functioning market:

IMPACT OF BLOCKCHAIN ON DIFFERENT MARKET PARTICIPANTS

DIMENSION	COMMENTS
Financial Guarantor	If the transaction is allowed to be T+0, as in no delay between the transaction confirmed to the chain and settlement of the transaction there is no timing risk thus no intermediary, other than the market itself, is required. However, in the US capital markets today there are legal mandates, not technological limitations, which set many settlement periods, such as the US equity market convention of T+3 which is set to move to T+2 by 3Q 2017[23]. If those settlement requirements remain then counterparties would be exposed to some risk. In these scenarios there is an opportunity to create some kind of holding account or have a clearing party serve the guarantor function.
Security Register and/or Transfer Agent	**Embedded Asset:** If the asset is embedded, for example through a digital equity issuance, then the marketplace will record and transfer the asset. A regulatory body could additionally receive information of the transaction directly to hold a consolidated, centralized view, to foster risk management.
	External Asset: If the asset is not built into the blockchain, then the record of the transaction will still be recorded. However, the transfer agent mechanism will need to be determined. The counterparties may decide where appropriate to transfer assets on their own, meeting agreed standards, or an intermediary could fill that role[24].

DIMENSION	COMMENTS
Technology Governing Body	The need for standards and protection of the blockchain infrastructure may dictate the need for its own oversight. Just as the internet saw the formation of such consortiums like ARIN (American Registry for Internet Numbers), IETF (Internet Engineering Task Force) and ICANN (Internet Corporation for Assigned Names and Numbers), an independent group of experts could help ensure stability, continued open source nature, and agree wider standards or changes.
Regulatory Oversight	While regulation and ensuring lawful compliance will still be a core concern to any market, blockchain could change the nature of regulatory oversight. This is because regulators will have greater transparency through the public nature of nodes within the network. The transparency blockchain has the ability to provide gives regulators a much clearer picture of what is going on in the markets on a close-to-real-time basis.

As some of these intermediary functions illustrate, the marketplace itself will absorb some of the roles currently. This adds a new dynamic to the idea of a market itself as an avenue for value creation. "Activity around blockchain technology is creating energy for further improvements to the system. A common barrier cited for some innovations is how to agree on a lead provider to hold central responsibility and power in an essentially monopolistic position. Perhaps the only way for the industry as a whole to agree who should develop such solutions is if they all collectively develop and own it together as in the case of blockchain."

An ability to unlock new business models also gives rise to the idea of a market on demand. As consumers have proven the value of the new shared economy model, an ability to build a market where trust, infrastructure costs and potentially geopolitical stability is not a roadblock means a big opportunity to design even more shared solutions. Markets could be thoughtfully designed with self-enforcing rules created through smart contracts, in areas where it wasn't possible before. One example would be to create a pool for individuals forced to self-insure. The question around markets may no longer be which market but rather what are the minimum viable characteristics for there to be a market.

Potential on-demand markets does not mean that traditional existing markets will have the same freedom to appear instantly. The minimum viable requirements for capital markets not only includes regulatory oversight but a significant pool of participants operating in the same space. Adam Ludwin at Chain estimates that despite many networks looking to launch, the lead institutions need others to join to stay viable. "I think there's a very real probability that only a handful of meaningful blockchain networks ultimately come to market and gain network effects, but that there are many, many participants on those networks."[25]

CHAPTER 3

Blockchain and Infrastructure (Identity, Data Security)

David Shrier, Weige Wu, Alex Pentland

I. INTRODUCTION: INFRASTRUCTURE (IDENTITY, DATA SECURITY)

We are living in a world that is rapidly undergoing a fundamental change: it is becoming driven by data. This is not just the Internet of Things (IoT) or ubiquitous mobile computing, this transformation is about all societal systems — traffic, health, government, logistics, marketing, power, defense — being qualitatively more quantified and efficient, but also more transparent and accountable. This changes not only the economics of systems, but their management and funding. It also blurs the lines between customer, citizen, company, and government. Everyone gets to see what is happening, and so everyone gets to have a role in shaping these new systems.

As a consequence, businesses in financial services, financial technology, software and security are struggling to understand what the changing landscape means and how they can participate. Not only is the technical environment changing quickly, but more importantly, as this new ecology develops the systems that support it will need to adapt rapidly as well. Recent data hacks such as Target and Ashley Madison reveal the dangers of a highly networked world in which our data is gathered and held in poorly-secured repositories.

Building an infrastructure that sustains a healthy, safe, and efficient society is, in part, a scientific and engineering challenge which dates back to the 1800s when the Industrial Revolution spurred rapid urban growth. That growth created new social and environmental problems. The remedy then was to build centralized networks that delivered clean water and safe food, enabled commerce, removed waste, provided energy, facilitated transportation, and offered access to centralized healthcare, police, and educational services. These networks formed the backbone of society as we know it today.

These century-old solutions are, however, becoming increasingly obsolete and inefficient. We now face the challenges of global warming, uncertain energy, water, and food supplies, and a rising population that will add 350 million people to the urban population by 2025 in China alone.[1] The new challenge is how to build an infrastructure that enables cities to be energy efficient, have secure food and water supplies, be protected from pandemics, and have better governance. Big data can enable us to achieve such goals. Rather than static systems separated by function – water, food, waste, transport, education, energy – we can instead regard the systems as dynamic, data-driven networks.

Instead of focusing only on access and distribution, we need networked and self-regulating systems, driven by the needs and preferences of citizens – a "nervous system" that maintains the stability of government, energy, and public health systems around the globe. A framework should be established which enables data to be captured about different situations, those observations to be combined with models of demand and dynamic reaction, and the resulting predictions to be used to tune the nervous system to match those needs and preferences.

Blockchain's highly resilient architecture and distributed nature make it an interesting platform to deliver this nervous system for society. In this chapter, we will explore applications of blockchain to identity and data security.

II. IDENTITY

Identity Authentication

The need for blockchain based identity authentication is particularly salient in the internet age. While there exists imperfect systems for establishing personal identity in the physical world, in the form of Social Security numbers, state liquor identification cards, drivers' licences and even passports or national identity cards, there is no equivalent system for securing either online authentication of our personal identities or the identity of digital entities. Facebook accounts, now often used as login for different digital applications, and media access control (MAC) addresses, may come close, yet both can hardly function as trustworthy forms of identification when they can be changed at will.

So while governments can issue forms of physical identification, online identities and digital entities do not recognize national boundaries and digital identity authentication appears at first look to be an intractable problem without an overseeing global entity. Yet it would be incredibly difficult, perhaps downright impossible, to establish a global entity overseeing digital identities given that there is common backlash against even national identity cards.[2] Blockchain technology may offer a way to circumvent this problem by delivering a secure solution without the need for a trusted, central authority.

Several blockchain startups are looking to use blockchain for online identity. A ShoCard, for example, is a digital identity that protects consumer privacy. ShoCard strives to be as easy to understand and use as showing a driver's license; and simultaneously be so secure that a bank can rely on it. The key is that the ShoCard Identity Platform is built on a public blockchain data layer, so as a company it is not storing data or keys that could be compromised. According to ShoCard all identity data is encrypted, hashed and stored in the blockchain, where it cannot be tampered with or altered. A start-up in a similar vein that bridges the gap of both human and digital entities, is Uniquid. Uniquid allows for the authentication of devices, cloud services, and people.[3] Uniquid's aim is to provide identity and access management of connected things, as well as humans, utilizing biometric information for the latter.

One implication of this trend for financial institutions is a growing need for improved identity authentication, particularly for compliance purposes. For compliance, blockchain technology may enable financial institutions to better verify customers during the onboarding process known as Know Your Client (KYC), and to better verify parties in a transaction and the transactions themselves to prevent fraudulent activities and more effectively comply with anti-money laundering (AML) regulation. Better AML/KYC systems can be used to help extend banking services to the world's 2 billion unbanked.

Privacy-Preserving Identity on Permissioned Blockchains

Increased transparency does not necessarily mean the end of privacy. Some cryptographic identity schemes offer strong privacy protection through identity anonymity and unlinkability of transactions. A new model for privacy-preserving identities is needed if blockchain systems are to operate at a global scale. It must allow entities in the ecosystem to (a) verify the "quality" or security of an identity, (b) assess the relative "freedom" or independence of an identity from any given authority (e.g. government, businesses, etc.), and (c) assess the source of trust for a digital identity. Yet, a part of identity is derived from physically identifying a person, and part is from their behaviors. As we allow for behavioral identity models, how can systems address people who behave inconsistently – perhaps, a good person who behaves badly sometimes? As people adopt digital avatars or personae, what is the identity that is being validated?

MIT researchers have proposed CoreID, a new means of establishing a trusted, yet privacy-preserving, identity. Designed for permissioned blockchains (such as those now being developed by several banks and trading platforms), the CoreID architecture adds an identity and privacy-preserving layer above the blockchain. An anonymous identity verification step allows anyone to read and verify transactions from the blockchain but only anonymous verified identities can have transactions processed. Economic incentives, similar to those used in mining itself, help create resiliency in the system to defend against attacks and preserve the integrity of the identity network.

This system creates the potential for compliance with AML/KYC regulations without compromising the individual identities of counterparties in a transaction.

Transaction Monitoring

According to a 2014 survey of compliance professionals by KPMG International, only 58% of respondents stated that their organization's transaction monitoring system is able to monitor transactions across different businesses, and only 53% said they could monitor across different jurisdictions.[4] Within financial institutions, blockchain technology offers a better data infrastructure, allowing for better quality, more comprehensive and potentially even lower-cost records. It is worth noting here that financial institutions will likely prefer permissioned rather than permissionless blockchain; this means that one of the two features of blockchain, that there is no need for a central authority, is to some extent eroded. In a typical permissioned blockchain, a central organization or uniform certification utility decides who is allowed to participate, thereby partially compromising the completely decentralized nature of permissionless blockchains. However, permissioned blockchains still offer the advantage of strong consensus security and financial institutions are actively investigating advantages and disadvantages of permissioned and permissionless blockchain databases.

Ownership Rights

The strong consensus security offered by blockchain without the need for a central certifying authority renders it particularly suitable for the authentication of ownership rights. This includes digital property, intellectual property and physical property, including physical products and land. For example, Ascribe is a startup in this space. It describes itself as a "fundamentally new way to lock in attribution, securely share and trace where digital work spreads". Ascribe creates a permanent and unbreakable link between the creator and his or her creative work. By allowing ownership to be forever verified and tracked, Ascribe leverages blockchain technology to make it possible to transfer, cosign or loan digital creations similar to physical pieces of work. By preventing unauthorized access to creative work, Ascribe also helps creators monetize their work.[5]

BlockVerify, on the other hand, is an example of a startup that utilizes blockchain to attribute intellectual property through verifying the provenance of luxury goods, physical products, and, addressing the issue of counterfeit goods by verifying the legal status of pharmaceuticals, diamonds and electronics.[6] In the public domain, blockchain can have profound effects on state maintained records as well. The Economist cites an example of Mariana Catalina Izaguirre, a resident in Teguciagalpa, Honduras, whose house was demolished when the records at the country's Property Institute did not reflect the official title which she had to the land.[7] In countries where data maintenance is poor and corruption rampant, blockchain offers a reliable alternative to current registries – because the history of transactions on blockchain are immutable, corrupt individuals cannot alter the records. This sort of security happens because blockchain is decentralized, so that it does not rely on a single authority for its maintenance, and therefore a single case of mismanagement causing a point of failure does not affect the accuracy of the records.

However, technology solutions are incomplete without integration into the fabric of society. If the genesis block is hard to establish, because, for example, many cousins could put a claim on the same property, no technology can resolve the dispute.

III. DATA SECURITY

Conventional models of data security rely on creating harder and harder "walls" – adding multiple factors to authentication for access and stronger encryption. They typically rely on the same fundamental concept: once you enter the system, you can access the data. Compartmentalization is typically minimal. Edward Snowden used a combination of social engineering and a low-tech "spider" to crawl over 1.7 million documents.[8] With blockchain, there exists the potential to "scatter the stack", rendering the cost of any one breach or combination of breaches much lower. Combined with strong encryption methods and zero knowledge proofs, a much more secure method of storing and accessing data can be established, enhancing the ability of data managers to protect critical information.

Decentralized Security

Underlying all of the above applications of blockchain technology is the importance of the data being securely held – in the sense that it cannot be tampered with. Data protection and privacy is another aspect of data security. The decentralized nature of blockchain may initially appear to be at odds with privacy; this is indeed a valid concern however there are some developments to reconcile the two. Enigma, for example, is a decentralized computation platform with guaranteed privacy, and an evolution upon the blockchain technology. Enigma's goal is to enable developers to build a 'privacy by design', end-to-end decentralized application without a trusted third party.[9]

Enigma is an extension of blockchain technology, because computation and data storage are not accomplished within the blockchain, instead the blockchain is an "operating system" for secure multiparty computations carried out by storage and computation nodes participating in the network. Data is split between different nodes, and different nodes cooperate to compute functions together without leaking information to the other nodes. In summary, "no single party ever has access to data in its entirety; instead, every party has a meaningless (i.e., seemingly random) piece of it."[10]

This essentially allows data to be used while its privacy is still guaranteed. Therefore, a program could be evaluated while the inputs are kept secret.[11] For example, it may be possible for the government to find out the characteristics of welfare recipients, and the type and amount of welfare support, without accessing the identities of the welfare recipients. Victims or whistleblowers can report crimes and have their claims verified without being identified by anyone.

Blockchain, distributed computation, and zero knowledge protocols, can help banks to solve numerous multi-jurisdiction data issues and capital calculations.

Besides Enigma, privacy is also a key concern within "traditional" blockchain technology. Storj is a peer-to-peer cloud storage network and claims to be the "most secure and private cloud".[12] Factom, the first usable blockchain technology to provide an unalterable record-keeping system, has partnered with medical records and services solutions provider, HealthNautica, to secure medical records and audit trails using the blockchain. By first cryptographically encoding private medical data, patient confidentiality is protected by ensuring that medical records are not revealed to third parties, including Factom, or transferred from their original location.[13]

IV. TOWARDS A NEW DEAL ON DATA

Blockchain holds the promise of enabling the "New Deal on Data": a greater degree of personal ownership, control, and monetization of personal data, within a framework that allows society to benefit from data aggregation. A simple example of the benefits of data aggregation is the traffic congestion information within Google Maps: by contributing location, speed of travel and other critical personal information, drivers gain the benefit of the common data pool in order to realize a shorter commute time and avoidance of traffic snarls. However, for this to happen, Google must aggregate personal location information about drivers. Imagine instead a system where you, the driver, have all of the benefits of pooled data but where you, not Google, owns and controls your own data. Based on quality and magnitude of contribution, you also may in future have the option to get paid for your effort of inputting data and aiding Google's commercial proposition.

The digital breadcrumbs we leave behind are clues to who we are, what we do, how we behave in different contexts, and what we want. This makes personal data – data about individuals – immensely valuable, both for public good and for private companies. As the European Consumer Commissioner, Meglena Kuneva, said recently, "Personal data is the new oil of the Internet and the new currency of the digital world."[14] The ability to see details of so many interactions is also immensely powerful and can be used for good or for ill. Therefore, protecting personal privacy and freedom is critical to our future success as a society. We need to enable more data sharing for the public good; at the same time, we need to do a much better job of protecting the privacy of individuals.

A successful data-driven society must be able to guarantee that our data will not be abused – perhaps especially that government will not abuse the power conferred by access to such fine-grained data. There are many ways in which abuses might be directly targeted – from imposing higher insurance rates based on individual shopping history,[15] to creating problems for the entire society, by limiting user choices and enclosing users in information bubbles.[16] To achieve the potential for a new society, we require the New Deal on Data, which describes workable guarantees that the data needed for public good are readily available while at the same time protecting the citizenry.[17]

The key insight behind the New Deal on Data is that our data is worth more when shared. Aggregate data – averaged, combined across population, and often distilled to high-level features – can be used to inform improvements in systems such as public health, transportation, and government. For instance, we have demonstrated that data about the way we behave and where we go can be used to minimize the spread of infectious disease.[18] Our research has shown how digital breadcrumbs can be used to track the spread of influenza from person to person on an individual level. And the public good can be served as a result: if we can see it, we can also stop it. Similarly, if we are worried about global warming, shared, aggregated data can reveal how patterns of mobility relate to productivity.[19] This, in turn, equips us to design cities that are more productive and, at the same time, more energy efficient. However, to obtain these results and make a greener world, we must be able to see people moving around; this depends on having many people willing to contribute their data, if only anonymously and in aggregate. In addition, the Big Data transformation can help society find efficient means of governance by providing tools to analyze and understand what needs to be done, and to reach consensus on how to do it. This goes beyond simply creating more communication platforms. The assumption that more interaction between users will produce better decisions may be very misleading. Although in recent years we have seen impressive uses of social networks for better organization in society, for example during political protests,[20] we are far from even starting to reach consensus about the big problems: epidemics, climate change, pollution – big data can help us achieve such goals.

However, to enable the sharing of personal data and experiences, we need secure technology and regulation that allows individuals to safely and conveniently share personal information with each other, with corporations, and with government. Consequently, the heart of the New Deal on Data must be to provide both regulatory standards and financial incentives enticing owners to share data, while at the same time serving the interests of individuals and society at large. We must promote greater idea flow among individuals, not just within corporations or government departments.

Personal Data as a New Asset Class

One of the first steps to promoting liquidity in land and commodity markets is to guarantee ownership rights so that people can safely buy and sell. Similarly, a first step toward creating more ideas and greater flow of ideas – idea liquidity – is to define ownership rights. The only politically viable course is to give individual citizens key rights over data that is about them, the type of rights that have undergirded the European Union's Privacy Directive since 1995.[21] We need to recognize personal data as a valuable asset of the individual, which can be given to companies and government in return for services.

We can draw the definition of ownership from English common law on ownership rights of possession, use, and disposal:

- You have the right to possess data about yourself. Regardless of what entity collects the data, the data belong to you, and you can access your data at any time. Data collectors thus play a role akin to a bank, managing data on behalf of their "customers".

- You have the right to full control over the use of your data. The terms of use must be opt in and clearly explained in plain language. If you are not happy with the way a company uses your data, you can remove the data, just as you would close your account with a bank that is not providing satisfactory service.
- You have the right to dispose of or distribute your data. You have the option to have data about you destroyed or redeployed elsewhere.

Individual rights to personal data must be balanced with the need of corporations and governments to use certain data- account activity, billing information, and the like to run their day-to-day operations. The New Deal on Data therefore gives individuals the right to possess, control, and dispose of copies of these required operational data, along with copies of the incidental data collected about the individual, such as location and similar context. These ownership rights are not exactly the same as literal ownership under modern law; the practical effect is that disputes are resolved in a different, simpler manner than would be the case for land ownership disputes, for example.

In 2007, one of the authors, Alex Pentland, first proposed the New Deal on Data to the World Economic Forum.[22] Since then, this idea has run through various discussions and eventually helped to shape the 2012 Consumer Data Bill of Rights in the United States, along with a matching declaration on Personal Data Rights in the European Union.

The World Economic Forum (WEF) echoed the European Consumer Commissioner Meglena Kuneva in dubbing personal data the "new oil" or new resource of the 21st century.[23] The "personal data sector" of the economy today is in its infancy, its state akin to the oil industry during the late 1890s. Productive collaboration between government (building the state-owned freeways), the private sector (mining and refining oil, building automobiles), and the citizens (the user-base of these services) allowed developed nations to expand their economies by creating new markets adjacent to the automobile and oil industries.

If personal data, as the new oil, is to reach its global economic potential, productive collaboration is needed between all stakeholders in the establishment of a personal data ecosystem. A number of fundamental uncertainties exist, however, about privacy, property, global governance, human rights – essentially about who should benefit from the products and services built on personal data.[24] The rapid rate of technological change and commercialization in the use of personal data is undermining end-user confidence and trust.

The current personal data ecosystem is feudal, fragmented, and inefficient. Too much leverage is currently accorded to service providers that enroll and register end-users. Their siloed repositories of personal data exemplify the fragmentation of the ecosystem, containing data of varying qualities; some are attributes of persons that are unverified, while others represent higher quality data that have been cross-correlated with other data points of the end-user. For many individuals, the risks and liabilities of the current ecosystem exceed the economic returns. Besides not having the infrastructure and tools to manage personal data, many end-users simply do not see the benefit of fully participating. Personal privacy concerns are thus addressed inadequately at best, or simply overlooked in the majority of cases. Current technologies and laws fall short of providing the legal and technical infrastructure needed to support a well-functioning digital economy.

Recently, we have seen the challenges, but also the feasibility of opening up private big data. In the Data for Development (D4D) Challenge (http:// www. d4d.orange.com), the telecommunication operator Orange opened access to a large dataset of call detail records from the Ivory Coast. Working with the data as part of a challenge, teams of researchers came up with life-changing insights for the country. For example, one team developed a model for how disease spreads in the country and demonstrated that information campaigns based on one-to-one phone conversations among members of social groups can be an effective countermeasure.[25] Data release must be carefully done, however; as we have seen in several cases, such as the Netflix Prize privacy disaster[26] and other similar privacy breaches,[27] true anonymization is extremely hard – recent research by de Montjoye et al. and others[28,29] has shown that even though human beings are highly predictable, we are also unique. Having access to one dataset may be enough to uniquely fingerprint someone based on just a few data points, and this fingerprint can be used to discover their true identity.

In releasing and analyzing the D4D data, the privacy of the people who generated the data was protected not only by technical means, such as removal of personally identifiable information (PII), but also by legal means, with the researchers signing an agreement that they would not use the data for re-identification or other nefarious purposes. Opening data from the silos by publishing static datasets – collected at some point and unchanging – is important, but it is only a beginning. We can do even more when data is available in real time and can become part of a society's nervous system. Epidemics can be monitored and prevented in real time,[30] underperforming students can be helped, and people with health risks can be treated before they get sick.[31]

The report of the World Economic Forum[32] suggests a way forward by identifying useful areas on which to focus efforts:

- Alignment of key stakeholders. Citizens, the private sector, and the public sector need to work in support of one another. Efforts such as NSTIC[33] in the United States – albeit still in its infancy – represent a promising direction for global collaboration.

- Viewing "data as money". There needs to be a new mindset, in which an individual's personal data items are viewed and treated in the same way as their money. These personal data items would reside in an "account" (like a bank account) where they would be controlled, managed, exchanged, and accounted for just as personal banking services operate today.

- End-user centricity. All entities in the ecosystem need to recognize end-users as vital and independent stakeholders in the co-creation and exchange of services and experiences. Efforts such as the User Managed Access (UMA) initiative[30] provide examples of system design that are user-centric and managed by the user.

When thinking about opportunity in the financial business space, entrepreneurs may wish to consider the potential of creating these new forms of data brokers – "data exchanges" that re-empower the individual and provide new revenue opportunities.

Securing the Trust Network

Blockchain holds the potential to unlock the prime requisite for a New Deal on Data: creating viable trust networks.

A "trust network" is a combination of networked computers and legal rules defining and governing expectations regarding data. For personal data, these networks of technical and legal rules keep track of user permissions for each piece of data and act as a legal contract, specifying what happens in case of a violation. For example, in a trust network all personal data can have attached labels specifying where the data comes from and what they can and cannot be used for. These labels are exactly matched by the terms in the legal contracts between all of the participants, stating penalties for not obeying them. The rules can – and often do – reference or require audits of relevant systems and data use, demonstrating how traditional internal controls can be leveraged as part of the transition to more novel trust models. A well-designed trust network, elegantly integrating computer and legal rules, allows automatic auditing of data use and allows individuals to change their permissions and withdraw data.

The mechanism for establishing and operating a trust network is to create system rules for the applications, service providers, data, and the users themselves. System rules are sometimes called "operating regulations" in the credit card context, "trust frameworks" in the identity federation context, or "trading partner agreements" in a supply value chain context. Several multiparty shared architectural and contractual rules create binding obligations and enforceable expectations on all participants in scalable networks. Furthermore, the design of the system rules allows participants to be widely distributed across heterogeneous business ownership boundaries, legal governance structures, and technical security domains. However, the parties need not conform in all or even most aspects of their basic roles, relationships, and activities in order to connect to a trust network. Cross-domain trusted systems must – by their nature – focus enforceable rules narrowly on commonly agreed items in order for that network to achieve its purpose.

By bringing the code to the data, as is common with the "smart contracts" capabilities of some blockchain systems, we can now embed the rules around data access and data governance directly within the network. The ability to realize the potential of creating greater authority of an individual over their own data is at hand.

CHAPTER 4

Mobile Money & Payments

David Shrier, German Canale, Alex Pentland

INTRODUCTION: MOBILE MONEY & PAYMENTS

Money is a medium dating back at least to Asia Minor in the 7th Century B.C.E. in the form of single-sided electrum coins issued by the Lydian Empire[1], and possibly earlier to clay tokens used by the Sumerian Empire in 8,000 B.C.E.[2]. If we expand the definition to include barter, we can date money back to 12,000 B.C.E. when obsidian and cattle served as media of exchange. Whether a social phenomenon that emerges and is subsequently regulated by governments (as the bitcoin ideologists would argue), or a means of control imposed from above by the State (as Prof. Christine Desan of Harvard Law argues[3]), today, money is undergoing a dramatic series of changes impelled by the adoption of an array of digital technologies. These changes in turn are driving an active dialog about the role of government in money, the opportunities for citizens to govern their own financial means of exchange, and the place technology holds in opening the Pandora's Box of monetary technology.

The growing ubiquity of mobile phones, in a number of emerging economies, is driving financial infrastructure to leapfrog developed nations, and is delivering a dynamic and changing sea of financial innovations. In China, Alibaba and WeChat are vying for primacy as the bank of the future. In the U.S., startups like Square and Looppay have provided new means of access for small merchants and individuals, increasing the potential for economic throughput in the small businesses that comprise a critical engine of economic growth.

We will explore, in this chapter, the terrain of mobile money and payments technology, the dynamics of the current system, and potential future areas for innovation.

I. DEFINITIONS OF MONEY

In a global world, why does geography matter so much for money?

Looking at recent developments in money, questions often arise about the difference between electronic money (e-money), mobile money, and a number of other terms used freely in this evolving space. While there may not be a universally agreed terminology, there has been general alignment among international organizations including the World Bank, GSMA and European Union, allowing us to start defining the terminology around digital money in a broadly accepted manner. For the purposes of this book we will use the below definitions.

Digital Money

We will use "digital money" as a catchall term to encompass e-money as well as mobile money. Technically, almost all money today is by definition "digital money", since once a deposit is made at a bank the "money" is converted into 1s and 0s. For our purposes, we will use digital money as an umbrella term for the new wave of innovative money access, transfer and management technologies.

e-money

Short for electronic money, the EU defines e-money as a monetary value represented by a claim on the issuer which is stored electronically and issued on receipt of funds, for the purpose of making payment transactions, and is accepted by natural or legal persons other than the issuer.[4] Under this definition e-money refers to any type of electronic stored value that serves as an alternative to cash. This could cover anything from gift cards to Bitcoin to values stored through Venmo. Traditionally e-money differs from money in a bank account in two significant ways. First, it is often not covered under financial protections such as the USA's FDIC insurance. Second it often does not earn interest.

Mobile Money

Mobile money refers to a broad spectrum of financial services which can be accessed through a mobile phone.[5] To date airtime purchases, bill payments and remittances are the leading uses of most mobile money services.[6] Mobile Banking, in contrast, specifically refers to the financial services associated with a bank account such as deposits, withdrawals or bill payments.

While mobile money can include access to e-money, surprisingly most mobile money services are still largely cash-based with service providers acting as intermediary cash agents. This partially explains why evolutions in mobile money are expected to contribute to financial inclusion. Of the 2.5 billion people as of 2012 that did not have a financial account, 1.7 billion had a mobile phone.[7] As of 2012 there were more mobile money accounts than traditional bank accounts in Kenya, Madagascar, Tanzania and Uganda.[8]

II. EVOLUTION OF MONEY TECHNOLOGY

When asked to picture money today, many people conjure up images of paper, metal, and plastic, yet with the rise of e-money and mobile banking this may soon be replaced with thoughts of a mobile app. While still in the early stages of service offerings, the rapidly growing societal acceptance of mobile money paves the way for new business models as well as raising fundamental questions about money and its relationship to technology, geography and financial access.

In some ways the newest developments in money represent a digital throwback to the early days of money with concepts like digital bartering, and currency that is based on an unregulated, individually agreed-upon value. Before laying out the potential impact mobile money could have, we will first develop a shared understanding of the definition of money and the evolution of money technology:

Money is any clearly identifiable object of value that is generally accepted as payment for goods, services and repayment of debts within a market or which functions in a manner similar to the legal tender of a country.

The earliest notions of money were associated with the barter systems that have existed almost as long as humanity itself. Aristotle in 350BC contemplated, "Of everything which we possess there are two uses: both belong to the thing as such, but not in the same manner, for one is the proper, and the other the improper or secondary use of it.
For example, a shoe is used for wear, and is used for exchange."[9] Barter systems had some key fundamental flaws, first it was subject to the coincidence of want's problem or the issue that trade was limited by the need for two parties with different goods that each wanted of the other's. Second all the parts of the transaction from sale, exchange and purchase were collapsed into one step.

Issues with bartering led to the first major evolution in money technology as a means of exchange and a store of value. This was a major step forward in convenience as money was now a unit of account.[10] An early coin currency was created in Lydia (now modern day Turkey) by King Alyattes in about 600 BCE. A century later China created the first paper currency, yet paper money did not gain significant popularity until 1661 AD in Sweden. These developments in money technology enabled many of the financial institutions we know today, ranging from banks to letters of credit, and increasing the fungibility and utility of money. Money remained relatively static until 1946 with the invention of the first modern credit card. The 1960s and 1970s brought computerization to retail banking with the advent of the ATM, promoted by John Reed at Citibank. The 1990s saw experimentation with a variety of digital currency technologies such as Flooz. 1999 saw the first mobile banking transactions through SMS by European Banks.[11] Interestingly enough, while mobile contactless payments are considered a very recent development, the origins of this type of payment was in 1997 with the "speedpass" payment system available at Mobil gas stations using RFID technology.[12]

In 2008, Satoshi Nakamoto introduced the world to Bitcoin, the first broadly-adopted, fully digital, decentralized cryptocurrency technology.[13] Sovereigns such as the China,[14] U.K.,[15] Japan,[16] even the Vatican[17] are exploring electronic versions of their own cryptocurrency and legitimizing digital currencies by incorporating into their existing regulatory schema, while offshore havens like Barbados[18] are both issuing fiat digital currency and avidly pursuing digital currency startups.

There are some important attributes for a store of value to be considered a valid currency. First, it is a medium of exchange agreed by a community of buyers and sellers. Second, it is in a form that is relatively efficient and convenient to exchange in the way that, for example, paper money is more favored than a gold brick. Lastly, it needs to be viewed as reliable. While short-run economic issues may occur, for a currency to have long-term staying power people must believe it will remain a store of value in the future.

Efficiency in exchange is deeply affected by money technology. Changes in efficiency both help drive the adoption of new money technologies as well as change people's spending behaviors.

One example is reflected in contactless payments. MasterCard published a study looking at 15 months' worth of spending habits based on enrollment in their PayPass program. The research showed that within the 12 months following their first contactless transaction, those accounts spent almost 30% more on average, using their PayPass-enabled card. This was true across the board when controlling for low, medium and high spending habits prior to enrollment. There was also a significant increase to top-of-wallet behaviors such as Recurring Payments, e-Commerce and Cross Border spend, with Cross Border spend exceeding a 50% increase in all three account types. According to Jonathan Orndorff, Principal at MasterCard Advisors and study lead, "In our highest spend segment, this lift translates into approximately $600 per month in incremental spend.[...] Lifts in not just overall spend but the quality of spend also helps the business case for contactless."[19]

Increasing efficiency encourages an increase in overall spending which is a strong motivator for financial and technology companies pursuing this goal. However, it raises interesting questions about an ideal level of ease of currency. Without a physical representation of money, will this lead to a loss of understanding of "value"? If spending is too easy, will this lead to a rise in negative financial behaviors such as overspending and impulse buying hurting long-term financial wellbeing?

Geography has also traditionally played a key role in currency, though often as a barrier for financial inclusion. Proximity was formerly a limiting factor to getting a sufficiently large market of buyers and sellers. For the third attribute of reliability to be ensured, government borders and national interests also became entangled with geography and with currency. This relationship has proven complex as geography and lack of proximity to financial institutions is one of the biggest impediments to increasing financial access.

Even as the world becomes increasingly interconnected, those without technological access, due to a physically remote location without sufficient infrastructure, or those who are prevented from obtaining access, become even more isolated from traditional banking systems, and more vulnerable to predatory practices. Mobile money through telecom networks can help bridge this last gap, so that technologies such as mobile money can be a key driver of economic growth and poverty alleviation. Better financial access can boost job creation, reduce economic vulnerability to shocks and increase investments in human capital. Far from a zero-sum game, financial inclusion has enormous impact potential from both a societal and revenue perspective. Within this chapter we will look at some ways groups are capitalizing on opportunities with mobile money and tapping into new customers, products and markets.

III. THE MOBILE MONEY ECOSYSTEM

"The three rules of retail are location, location, location. In mobile money, they're partnership, partnership, partnership. We need to create a mesh of partnerships covering various networks of relationships."[20] As Napoleon Nazareno, President of Smart Communications highlights, a high degree of network interconnectivity is critical to the mobile money ecosystem. To that end, it is evolving at a global scale with many players, large and small as well as traditional and new entrants. While networks are a critical component to the landscape, traditional industry lines are increasingly blurring, particularly between mobile service providers and finance, bringing opportunities for new business models but also bringing competitive threats from unexpected industries. Some of the key roles from an end to end perspective include, though are not limited to:

When these players collaborate, the results can drive significant change. The M-Pesa, an e-money and mobile product offering of the Kenyan Pesa, has driven meaningful adoption. As of 2013, 93% of the adult population in Kenya is registered for M-Pesa and 60% actively use the service. The impact of the M-Pesa is much broader as it has facilitated the creation of thousands of small businesses and gave nearly 20 million Kenyans access to financial services, particularly low-income Kenyans. The percentage of people living on less than $1.25 a day using M-Pesa grew from less than 20% in 2008 to 72% in three years.[21]

M-Pesa's origins were in research. The UK's Department for International Development (DFID), noticed that Kenyans were bartering mobile airtime as an alternative to cash. DFID saw the unserved need and connected with communications service provider Vodafone, who was looking for opportunities to support microfinance through its mobile platform. Vodafone and DFID each made matching investments of £1 million. MNOs have been able to become fast movers in the mobile money space through their greater levels of investment and their existing networks and distribution channels. According to the Global Mobile Systems Association, in 2014 there were 255 mobile money services across 89 countries, including 60% in developing markets.

The M-Pesa also highlights some tension between these players, specifically MNOs and finance companies. While MNOs have taken a step into finance, finance companies are starting to return the favor. Safaricom has enjoyed an almost monopoly as the sole authorized mobile money services provider. In 2014 three more MNOs were authorized, including Kenya's most profitable bank Equity Group, all of which use Safaricom's largest competitor Airtel's mobile network. Equity Group started offering free SIM cards to drive adoption and acquired more than 650,000 customers by mid-2015. Bitcoin-based competitors like Bitpesa are gaining market share. While M-Pesa still holds 20 million out of the 26 million mobile consumers in Kenya, the competition is starting which will serve both the private and public good.[22]

As discussed earlier, the majority of mobile transactions still involve some component of cash. This puts a spotlight on two of the players, employers and agents. There is a clear use case for retailers to accept mobile payments but employers offering mobile payment of wages is still less understood and still a nascent area. According to the World Bank just over 1% of all employees received money through phones. One notable regional exception is the developing nations of Sub-Saharan Africa, where 7.8% of employees receive wages through phones.[23] Why this is significant becomes apparent when you look at the striking difference in cash versus direct transfers into a financial account between low income and high income groups. A comparison chart is included below. Cash wages present risks not just to employees but also employers. Moving to a mobile system reduces the need to keep cash on hand or make bank trips, both of which have a higher theft risk as well as a more efficient and trackable way to manage payroll. Retailers who can already benefit from adoption of mobile payments can continue to leverage these services further to the benefit of their employees.

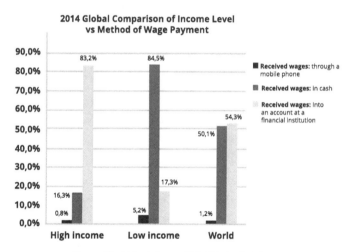

Source: World Bank Group. Global Findex Database.

Agents' role in the ecosystem should not be understated, particularly in developing countries. Agents are contracted by mobile money service providers to facilitate transactions for users. A 2012 McKinsey study of mobile money providers in emerging markets looking at why many solutions failed to gain sustainable scale and identified that execution was the problem. More specifically, poor agent networks was the largest factor, with a need for compelling product offerings and maintained corporate commitment as other key factors.[24] Often it is believed that agents' most important function is cashing-in and out for clients. Liquidity, both in terms of physical cash and e-float, are often limiting factors for clients. Similarly, liquidity is a challenge for agents and so a super-agent, or larger intermediary agent, is required. While liquidity is a current barrier, these are surmountable logistics issues.

Arguably the agents' other role as an extension of their primary retail business is far more important. They are in essence front-line customer service, as a result they are make-or-break for company trust and customer education, both of which directly impact activity rates. Yet agents are often not trained or incentivized for such a role. The Gates Foundation estimates that agents must process around 30 to 50 transactions per day for their business to be viable because most are paid on commission. It could take upwards of a year for an agent to make a profit so typically agents also have other kinds of business in addition to mobile money. This means the person teaching new mobile money clients how to use the mobile services is at best part-time and at worst misleading clients while pushing other sales. Different countries have different regulations for agents, highlighting another difficult aspect of mobile money regulation. With a global ecosystem comes a global array of regulators.

"When regulators embrace a leadership role in developing the market, they become innovative and take reasonable risks inherent to making the changes needed to create a more inclusive financial sector. Although regulators' main concern is always the safety and soundness of financial systems, those that have made the most progress have been willing to explore new routes or to use new tools to enhance traditional financial activities."[25]

As expressed by Professor Prof. Njuguna Ndung'u, governor of the Central Bank of Kenya, the responsibilities for regulators fall under two umbrella concepts, protection and innovation facilitation. While the need to protect is always important, regulators have an opportunity to make a huge difference to financial inclusion and economic prosperity not just with mobile money but with development of the broader range of new financial technologies. Innovation facilitation in this area involves a focus on interoperability and becoming leaders in global collaboration.

Regulators will need to grapple with new issues such as having a stance on e-money and dealing with financial or adjacent products created by non-banks. Areas that used to have clear functions, like a bank and a telecommunications provider, had clear and expert governing regulatory bodies. Regulation will need to span not just across industry but now across borders. Cross border payments and products are increasingly highlighting the need for more coordinated regulation both for technology standards and policy. This collaboration requires careful balancing with national interests.

There has been promising headway. In 2013 the Financial Action Task Force (FATF), the inter-governmental group developing policies to fight money laundering and terrorist financing, issued its first-ever guidance document for prepaid cards, mobile payments and internet based payment services. It takes a risk-based approach and covers almost all big mobile money markets, from Kenya to Pakistan, where these types of risks are highest. The FATF left significant leeway for national regulators to regulate mobile money services in a way they saw best fit to promote financial inclusion and innovation.

With a cohesive regulatory environment, the range of transaction and services for which mobile money can be used will eventually be as broad as financial services that exist today. A prime example of this are credit score ratings. The traditional credit score is based, in part, on having credit already – an inherent obstacle to financial access (if you don't have credit, you can't get credit). Our group at MIT wanted to see if using mobility data (how people move around and where they shop) could better predict the likelihood of someone experiencing financial difficulties in the future, such as overdrawing on an account or missing a payment.

Analyzing hundreds of thousands of transactions using financial and location (mobile geography information) the team created a predictive model based on animal foraging and behavior patterns resulting in models that were 30-49% better at predicting financial distress than traditional demographic models.[26] Understanding client's behaviors in a deeper way means that a bank could work with the client before financial hardship and help them make better financial decisions.

IV. MOBILE TRADING

Through mobile trading, investors are able to access trading platforms from smartphones as opposed to only on their computers or through direct communication with brokers. Mobile trading is a natural extension that follows on from online trading, as mobile becomes the dominant channel for internet access. According to Ofcom Technology in 2015, 33% of internet connections occurred through smartphones, followed by laptops at 30%, tablets at 19% and desktops at 14%.[27]

In 1982, the first full service electronic consumer equity trading system called NAICO-NET, offered by North American Holding Corp., for buying and selling stocks, mutual funds and commodities on a computer came online.[28] TradePlus was founded by William Porter and Bernard Newcomb around the same time, and offered a retail trading platform in 1985. The same founders subsequently founded E-trade in 1991, which offered trading services via America Online and Compuserve. E-trade has offered mobile trading platforms since 2010 and has a market capitalization of nearly $7 billion US dollars today.

The 1990s saw other retail brokers, such as Charles Schwab and TD Ameritrade, launch in the online market.[29] Today, although the traditional players such as Charles Schwab, TD Ameritrade, Fidelity and Merrill Edge remain dominant players in the mobile trading industry, recent start-ups have introduced further innovations. We see four key trends across the online retail trading industry: namely the proliferation of (i) mobile apps, (ii) greater access through lower fees and barriers to entry, (iii) social functionality and crowdsourced information sources, (iv) greater sophistication in functionalities. Some examples include:

- **Mobile apps:** All of the four traditional players mentioned above offer mobile apps. Offering mobile functionality is becoming the industry norm for retail online brokerage firms. A recent study conducted by ORC International for Fidelity revealed that 56% of mobile users access financial apps for sophisticated investing tasks such as analysis, reports, and trading.[30] Mobile trades comprised 5.5% of all retail trades placed in December 2013, but exceeded 7% in December 2014, showing a gain of 43.7%.[31]

- **Greater access through lower fees and barriers to entry:** Robinhood, for example, offers commission-free trading on U.S.-listed stocks and exchange-traded funds (ETFs), as opposed to $6.99 to $9.99 per trade for the traditional players.

- **Social functionality and crowd-sourced information:** Estimize[32] and Vetr[33] are examples of companies which provide crowd-sourced ratings and data for the stock market.

- **Increased sophistication in functionality:** Motif Investing helps facilitate the building of thematic portfolios.[34]

The three largest online brokers, Charles Schwab[35], E*TRADE[36] and TD Ameritrade[37] collectively control over $3.6 trillion in assets across 20 million accounts as of April 2016. However, the industry is undergoing fragmentation, with margins being squeezed further by no-commission online brokers, such as Robinhood and Loyal3.

Robinhood, which has raised over $66 million of venture funding, plans to make money off margin accounts (accounts where investors borrow money to buy securities), currently testing in beta mode, and interest accrual from customers' uninvested cash balances.[38]

Motif Investing, backed by $126.5 million, allows investing at commission of $9.95 per motif and $4.95 per single stock. Fidelity, Charles Schwab, and Ameritrade charge commission of between $7.95-$9.95 per trade.[39]

Feex is a startup that exposes "hidden fees" in financial services (particularly asset management), and is seeking to recover a claimed $600 billion annually from incumbent financial services providers.[40] Decision analytics tools like these will become increasingly important as consumers become more sophisticated.

As we explore beyond trading platforms into advisory tech, Personal Capital, Wealthfront and Betterment have created great unease within the traditional wealth and asset management firms with their Millennial-friendly approach. In the summer of 2015, BlackRock purchased FutureAdvisor to stay competitive in this dynamically evolving landscape.[41]

We will explore Robo-advising in more detail in our forthcoming paper "Artificial Intelligence & Financial Services".

V. MONEY TRANSFERS

Online peer-to-peer money transfers allow consumers to quickly and easily send money to each other, without having to deal with the cumbersome process of writing and mailing a check or transferring physical cash. Online money transfers are not characterized by the location where the consumer authorizes the transfer; paying rent to a US-based roommate on an app works exactly the same way whether one is in the next room or thousands of miles away – as long as there is an internet connection and perhaps international mobile roaming for authorization purposes. We will first explore peer-to-peer money transfers in general, and then move on to international remittances in particular in the next section.

PayPal is often associated with the ushering of the new online peer-to-peer payments era in the 2000s. Now, many traditional banks offer a way to do this easily online. Bank of America, for example, allows its customers to send money to friends using just a phone number or email address of the receiving party.[42] Outside of traditional banks, platforms from fintech and consumer tech players offer peer-to-peer payment options that are often well integrated into messaging or other social functionalities.

PayPal's founders came together in 1998 and started an online company X.com, with PayPal soon emerging as the chief focus of the company. PayPal quickly identified an opportunity with online marketplaces, which clearly required a way for consumers to quickly and safely transfer money online. In 2000, PayPal partnered with eBay, and its account base rose to 100,000.[43] Today, PayPal has 184 million active customer accounts, is available to people in more than 200 markets, and allows customers to get paid in more than 100 currencies.[44] Peer-to-peer payments are free on PayPal and it earns its revenue through charging merchants for virtual purchases by consumers.

Now, PayPal is being disrupted by other entrants offering "digital wallets". Venmo is a free digital wallet that lets one make and share payments with friends. It is quite clearly targeted at Millennials – the age group most likely to be splitting restaurant and cab bills – and offers social functionality where one can share one's payments on a page that is similar to the "wall" on Facebook. In 2012, Venmo was acquired by Braintree for $26 million, and just a year later Braintree was acquired by PayPal for $800 million.[45]

Outside of fintech companies, consumer tech companies are also eyeing the peer-to-peer payments space as a gateway into the general online payments space. WeChat, a wildly popular social messaging app with many other integrated features including mobile payments, has 700 million monthly active users, out of which 200 million are linked to bank accounts.[46] Facebook is following this example and rolled out peer-to-peer payments through messages in 2015[47], while fellow tech giant Google offers the Google Wallet, allowing instant peer-to-peer payments using an email address or phone number[48].

In the US, many of the peer-to-peer payments platforms are free. Monetization mainly comes through helping consumers connect with businesses. Peer-to-peer payments is a customer acquisition strategy that allows the platform to capture sign-ups easily, and the platform can then be used for purchases from merchants. WeChat already allows users to make payments online with participating retailers[49], and Venmo allows payments to merchants after its acquisition by PayPal.[50] Other platforms are likely to move into this direction.

The trend of integration of payments into messaging apps will also continue. As online peer-to-peer payments become even more accessible from different social platforms, peer-to-peer payments may become more of an extension of communication between friends, and integrated into social sharing capabilities as with Venmo.

VI. INTERNATIONAL REMITTANCES

According to the World Bank, migrants send back earnings to their families at levels above US$441 billion, a figure three times the volume of official aid flows. These inflows of cash constitute more than 10% of GDP in 25 developing countries. The top recipient countries of recorded remittances in 2015 are India, China, the Philippines, Mexico, and France, and the top source countries are the United States (US), Saudi Arabia, Russia, Switzerland and Germany. The top remittance corridors are US to Mexico ($25.2B), US to China ($16.3B) and Hong Kong SAR to China ($15.6B).[51]

Remittance here refers to a broad range of transactions, which includes personal transfers, compensation of employees, capital transfers between households,
and social benefits, with personal transfers including all transfers from/ to resident to/from nonresident households regardless of whether the recipient is a family member or not.[52] This means that remittances constitute a large component of all consumer-to-consumer international money transfers and will be the focus of this section.

The international money transfer players include banks, money transfer companies with physical branches such as Western Union and Moneygram, and fintech start-ups utilizing online and mobile platforms. Traditionally, money transfer companies have a physical network of branches, which may be at banks, post offices or shops, and agents within local communities which act as the conduits for money transfers.

According to one report, fintech start-ups are able to charge a quarter of the average price for remittance compared to banks, thus gaining a strategic advantage and posing steep price competition in the industry. Costs are reduced primarily by doing away from overhead from brick and mortar operations. Given that money transfer costs exceed 10% to 20% of the money transfer, there is still tremendous opportunity for disruption.[53]

Technological innovation in infrastructure can also decrease the amount of time for transfers and correspondingly the amount of liability money transfer companies have to bear if money is sent to the recipient before the company receives it. The Ripple protocol, for example, is an open source distributed ledger (blockchain) application that functions as a payment network that supports a variety of currency exchanges. This protocol allows for the exchange of value in real time, as opposed to a day to clear on the ACH network.[54]

However, fraud and compliance issues impose huge costs on fintech startups and traditional money transfer companies alike. Inigio Rumayor, founder of Regalii, a one-stop API for global bill management, lists online fraud as the number one concern that he has encountered. Fraud in money transfer is particularly lucrative, and many money transfer companies offering quick or "instant transfers" often incur a huge liability because money may be sent to the recipient before the money transfer company receives it.[55] Fraud issues are not exclusive to online or mobile set-ups – Western Union lists the types of scams on its website, specifically listing that fraudsters can make contact through telephone or physical surface mail.[56]

Compliance costs may also be a large burden to start-ups. Start-ups in the US, for example, not only need to comply with federal regulations but also state regulations. This means that it may take two years and three million dollars to simply be registered as a money transfer company.[57]

One example of a success story with great social impact is Sendwave. Sendwave allows instant, no-fee transfers from US and Canada to Africa. This is an extremely timely innovation especially given that money transfers to Sub-Saharan Africa remain extremely expensive at an average of 9.53%.[58] While companies such as Western Union and MoneyGram make money on both exchange and fees, Sendwave only makes money on an exchange rate. By offering an online service and saving on physical infrastructure and other costs, Sendwave claims to save its customers $9 on every $100 transfer.[59] Given that money transfers are common within the low-income population, lowering the costs of remittance can increase the effective purchasing power of receiving families back home.

Similarly, B2B companies may also be successful by providing supporting infrastructure. CurrencyCloud is a UK-based provider of cross-boundary money transfer services and has raised $35 million. It counts Azimo, TransferWise and xe.com among its customers.[60]

Because of cybersecurity challenges and compliance costs, new fintech players aiming to compete on costs face low margins. It remains to be seen which fintech players become dominant players comparable to Western Union and MoneyGram.

VII. MOBILE PAYMENTS

When a payment is made under financial regulation and performed from a mobile device, we refer to it as a mobile payment. Instead of paying with bills, coins, cards or checks, consumers use their mobile device (generally, smartphones) to pay for goods and services.

In addition to the obvious convenience for users (both consumers and firms), this type of payment introduces a huge problem for multiple non-banking companies (from Amazon to Apple and AT&T) that currently have more direct access to transaction data from millions of consumers. This transaction data is extremely valuable, both because firms can use it to increase profits and governments need such data for regulation and tax purposes.

Companies can profit from this trend in multiple ways. Here are some success stories that exemplify some of the ways on which firms have thrived in the mobile payments arena.

- Big companies like Google have entered the arena. In this case, the Mountain View-based giant created Google Wallet, trying to become your go-to mobile payments platform. As in most projects where Google is involved, the biggest value comes not from the operation per se but from the data that such an operation generates.
- Medium-sized companies like Domino's Pizza have also entered the arena. In the case of most retailers, the goal is to facilitate mobile-based consumption. Now, you can order a pizza and pay for it in a matter of seconds. Naturally, the impact is to defend (and ideally increase) market share, revenues and profits by leveraging technology.

- Startup companies like Venmo are created with the sole intention to play in this field. This firm's solution became a convenient way to collect and pay money among friends, and thus attracted acquirers – Braintree bought Venmo in 2012 and then PayPal acquired Braintree in 2013. Six months ago, PayPal announced that it plans to let merchants accept payments through Venmo.

Companies from all sizes are entering this field. Some enter by creating new business units (e.g., Google), others by innovations that complement their current operations (e.g., Domino's) and yet others to be acquired by larger organizations or investment firms (e.g., Venmo).

VIII. EXTRAPOLATING THE NEAR FUTURE

"We've entered the most profound era of change for financial services companies since the 1970s brought us index mutual funds, discount brokers and ATMs" – B.I. Intelligence[61]

Incumbents and new entrants into the financial ecosystem are entering into a period of vigorous competition, fueled by technology disruption and consumer adoption. To illustrate some of these battles, we are already seeing a battle between i) traditional banks and online-only banks, ii) retail lenders and peer-to-peer marketplaces, and iii) old-school asset managers and robo-advisors. In each of these three battles, there will be winners and losers on both sides of the table as no enterprise is immune and all firms need to harness the power of new financial technologies. Bitcoin, the first blockchain-based currency, has spread faster than almost any other technology – even the World Wide Web or mobile broadband. Bitcoin was not the first cryptocurrency, and will likely not be the last one. According to Bitcoin Magazine, the very first attempt at cryptocurrencies took place in the Netherlands, in the 1980s[62]. Yet it is safe to say that Bitcoin is now the most recognized and used cryptocurrency of all of this new generation of cryptocurrencies.

In chapter 1, we discussed the fundamentals of the technology behind Bitcoin. Blockchain represents a technology innovation that enables transparent interactions of parties on a more trusted and secure network which distributes access to data:

- It has the potential to disrupt not only the financial services industry but also many more, including healthcare, logistics and real estate.
- Venture investment in the Blockchain field was $1 billion in 2015 and is expected to grow to $10 billion in 2016[63].

We envision a near future where Blockchain-based currencies are adopted by millions of people across industries and geographies. It may or may not be a modified form of Bitcoin: there are a number of regulatory and functional challenges inherent in Bitcoin's current iteration. A large number of developers and entrepreneurs are working to address them.

At the same time, central banks are contemplating issuance of cryptocurrency. The implications of this are manifold, and include a fundamental thread to the financial foundations of extant commercial banks (if you don't need to deposit money into a bank to receive the right to transfer money electronically, but instead can directly transfer money using "Britcoin", the British commercial banks lose an incredibly cheap source of financing: customer deposits).

Aside from cryptocurrencies, the list of other forms of money includes – but is not limited to:

a) Airtime: the use of pre-paid mobile-phone minutes as currency, such as by MIT spinoff company Jana Communications;

b) Gift cards: pre-paid coupons that can be interchanged for products and/or services at selected companies; and

c) Loyalty program-based points: accumulated benefits that can be converted into money for selected brands and firms that compose the group.

These alternative forms of money are still widely used globally. According to The Economist, "Pre-paid minutes can be swapped for cash or spent in shops most easily in Côte d'Ivoire, Egypt, Ghana and Uganda"[64]. Popular retailers, including Banana Republic, Macy's, and Victoria's Secret still heavily promote gift cards. And airlines not only keep on promoting loyalty programs but also push for integration with other companies, so that you can use your flight miles to buy hotel nights, among many other things.

Yet, none of these have come close to the disruption that new-generation cryptocurrencies have introduced.

"There is a very real danger that financial regulation will become a wolf in sheep's clothing" - Henry Paulson

It is not the intention of this document to discuss public policy. Nevertheless, it is important to highlight the double challenge that governments face around mobile payments. On the one hand, regulators need to create a norm that satisfies the rule of law and is fair to society. On the other hand, they cannot block innovation. How to balance these two is neither easy nor static, in a sector that is particularly dynamic.

We believe that mobile money and the rest of the fintech revolution will ultimately alter every industry in the economy. Over the following months and years, we expect this to be particularly true around the financial services sectors: payments, lending, retail and institutional banking, asset management, insurance, and markets/exchanges.

Mobile money has introduced a business model that works for mass-markets: high volume and low margins. And as the number of smartphones increases on a daily basis, so does the number of potential mobile money users[65]. With 500 million smartphones anticipated to be deployed in Africa by 2020 (80% of them over the next few years), transformational change to the "last frontier market" is potentially at hand[66].

Entrepreneurial action holds the potential to lead the disruption of the financial ecosystem and deliver better service, at better prices, to consumers. This will come at the cost of stability to the incumbent banks and other financial services market participants. As a consequence we leave you with this question: how can we navigate this disruption with the least harm to society?

CHAPTER 5

Prediction Markets

David Shrier, Dhaval Adjodah,
Weige Wu, Alex Pentland

I. THE FIRST BULL (OX) MARKET

Introduction

Prediction markets are a powerful means of harnessing network intelligence to predict future events. In the mid 2000's, there was a period of excitement around their potential that faded when confronted with poor accuracy and reliability. New developments in human-machine systems inspire us to revisit the topic.

Origins of Prediction Markets

In 1906, Francis Galton, half-cousin of Charles Darwin, and a polymath who created the statistical concept of correlation, observed a weight-judging competition in Plymouth, England. Eight hundred competitors bought stamped and numbered cards for 6 pence to inscribe their estimate of the weight of a chosen ox[1]. Galton observed that the average competitor, who is not likely to be an expert in oxen, was as well-equipped to make a fair estimate of the ox as the average voter is capable of judging the merits of most political issues on which he or she votes[2]. To his surprise, the vox populi, or voice of the people, was astonishingly accurate – the median was within 0.8% of the true weight[3], and the average within 0.08%[4]. Galton concluded that the result is more favorable to the credibility of a democratic judgment than he might have expected[5], and this story became immortalized as an early example of what we now call the "wisdom of the crowds".

Galton's Ox offers a glimpse of the concept that the aggregation of the opinions of many people can be surprisingly good predictors of outcomes, even where most of the individuals are not who we traditionally consider experts. This "wisdom of the crowds" shall emerge as a dominant theme as we explore the development of prediction markets.

Definition of Prediction Markets

Prediction markets are markets that involve making forecasts about states of the future, using predictive analytics. Here, we employ a broad definition. The term prediction market is sometimes used to refer to only markets forecasting outcomes of events, and in this chapter we include forecasting of prices of different assets, such as futures markets and hedge funds that specialize in identifying patterns and predicting price movements.

Political prediction markets date back to the sixteenth century, when betting on the next pope was considered common practice and banned by Pop Gregory XIV in 1591[6]. Gambling odds were printed daily in newspapers such as the New York Times in the early twentieth century. They only declined in popularity due to the advent of scientific pooling[7] before interest was again re-kindled in this area.

Present-day examples include Iowa Electronic Markets, which has allowed students from participating institutions to invest and trade in a variety of contracts since 1998. Students make predictions on future events by buying shares in their outcomes, with the price an indication of the probability that the event will occur. While trading relating to outcomes of political processes are most well-known, students can also trade in a corporation's stock price, quarterly earnings, or movie's box office receipts[8]. PredictIt operates similarly to allow users, who need not be students, to buy shares in outcomes of future political events such as whether the Brexit, OPEC quota reduction, or North Korea hydrogen bomb test will happen[9].

Futures markets, which involve prices of real underlying assets, rather than probabilities of events, originated in the 1730s in Japan. Samurai were paid in rice, and the purchasing power of their income was strained when good rice harvests brought down the price of rice, leading to the first creation of rice bills. The first futures exchange, the Chicago Board of Trade, emerged a century later in 1848[10]. Futures markets of real underlying assets or their prices may also contain information about probabilities of future events. In 1984, economists studied the relationship between orange futures and the weather. Orange trees cannot withstand freezing temperatures for over a few hours, and the paper found that the prices of orange futures at the close of market at 2.45pm, predicted errors in the weather forecasts of the minimum temperature later that evening. This serves as an illustration of how the crowd, in this case the aggregation of orange buyers and suppliers, may end up revealing information about the weather that even the weather experts miss[11].

Mechanisms of Action

This leads us to the questions: Why do prediction markets work? Is this merely a coincidence or are there underlying reasons? The market mechanism naturally aggregates information of prices, as a transaction happens only when there is a willing buyer and seller at that price. There is a monetary incentive to reveal the truth because of potential gains[12]. In addition, there are long-term incentives for specialization in discovering new information and to trade on it[13]. The markets themselves can do a better job of predicting prices when the prediction errors of each individual are distributed symmetrically around the true value, and with finite variance, so law of large numbers applies. This is known in probability theory as an application of the central limit theorem.

AI and Prediction Markets

Recent advances in artificial intelligence means that, beyond the crowd, advanced artificial intelligence techniques are also used to predict outcomes. This does not imply that artificial intelligence would leave wisdom of the crowds obsolete in the near future though. In 2016 we saw a breakthrough in artificial intelligence when Google's artificial intelligence AlphaGo defeated world champion, Lee Sedol, at the game "Go". "Go" is a 2,500 year-old game that is said to be exponentially more complex than chess and requires an added degree of intuition[14]. But we are reminded of the 'centaurs' – human-computer hybrid teams – that rose after the defeat of chess world champion Garry Kasparov by IBM's Deep Blue in 1997. Comparative chess amateurs Steven Cramton and Zackary Stephen, whose world rankings hovered around 1,400 to 1,700, won the freestyle chess tournament in 2005, beating Hydra, the most powerful chess computer at that time, using regular Dell and Hewlett-Packard computers and software that can be purchased for sixty dollars[15]. This reveals the power of human-computer collaboration, where a computer's ability to process large amounts of data reliably combines with human intuition and empathy to outdo what either man or machine could have achieved on their own.

II. PEAK OF HYPE, CRASH, FIZZLE AND REBIRTH

Prediction markets are only just emerging from the trough of disillusionment in the Gartner Hype Cycle, as illustrated by our adaptation of their 2015 report:

EMERGING TECHNOLOGY HYPE CYCLE

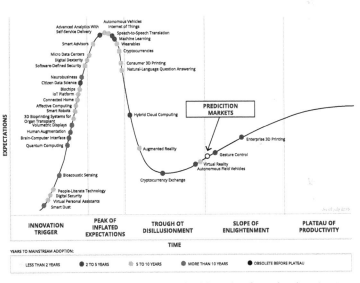

The Gartner Hype cycle breaks down the life cycle of a technology into five phrases. First is a technology breakthrough, which triggers media interest and publicity. Early publicity, fueled by a small number of success stories, generates excitement, leading to the peak of inflated expectations in the second stage. As failures of these exaggerated expectations occur, the technology enters the trough of disillusionment in the third stage, with investments continuing only if surviving providers improve products to the satisfaction of the early adopters[16].

This is followed by the fourth stage of the slope of enlightenment, where the technology matures. During this phase, more benefits and use cases are found, and second-and third-generation products emerge. The fifth and last stage is the plateau of productivity, where mainstream adoption takes off[17].

Proliferation of Predictions

Prediction markets have existed for centuries and, while there was no single technology breakthrough that could be responsible for its increase in popularity, the rise of a more networked society (greater connectivity among predictors) and better software and hardware systems to manage this connectivity was undoubtedly a contributing factor.

In the early- to mid- 2000s, uses of prediction markets begun to proliferate, leading to the second stage peak of inflated expectations. After they accurately forecasted events from sales of computer printers to election results and the Federal Reserve's interest rate decisions, prediction markets were even used to forecast the spread of infectious diseases[18]. In 2001, the Defense Advanced Research Project Agency (DARPA) also started experimenting with prediction markets to forecast terrorism; only to have the program cancelled in 2003 under congressional criticism[19].

Dawning Disillusionment

Criticism of prediction markets came to a head around 2008. This could be seen as the ushering in of the third stage of the trough of disillusionment. When Obama did not win the California primary after Intrade, a prediction market founded in 1999, criticism emerged. Prediction markets were said to be too small, the stakes too low, and too slow to react to events[20]. Intrade also gave an 80% chance that the Supreme Court would overturn Obama's health care law, which did not materialize. Even then, however, it was recognized that Intrade's record is better than that of any single poll or pundit.[21] After all, if prediction markets gave an 80%-certain prediction, then it should be wrong one out of every five times. True to Gartner's Hype cycle, prediction markets could not meet some of the then-inflated expectations.

The trough of disillusionment was intensified by the collapse of Intrade. This is significant because at that time, Intrade was the only real-money prediction market focused on forecasting the likelihood of events. The Dodd-Frank financial reform signed by President Obama in 2010 bans futures related to terrorism, assassination, gaming, and anything "contrary to the public interest", advising in 2012 that elections are covered. A Commodities Futures Trading Commission (CFTC) spokesperson declined to comment on Intrade. Then in 2012 the 'Romney Whale' appeared. The 'Romney Whale' added $3.8 million to an already enormous bet on Romney even as polls swung towards Obama, causing Intrade to put Obama's price at 70 when an Obama victory was almost assured and quoted as 90% in the New York Times[22]. This raised suspicions that the price was being manipulated for political reasons. Separately, the CFTC sued Intrade citing its decision to return to offering markets on financial predictions like the future unemployment rate. Intrade suspended operations in March 2013 and financial discrepancies including $4.2 million missing in accounts from Intrade and a related company surfaced.[23]

Innovation-Fueled Rebirth

Since then, however, it has begun to appear that we are moving into the fourth Hype cycle stage of maturation of technologies, such as quadratic voting. Under quadratic voting, individuals buy votes in favor of their preferred alternative from a clearing house, paying the square of the number of votes purchased. Economists have recently shown that this mechanism ensures efficient outcomes in large populations[24]. Other innovations include incorporating information about the prior quality of predictions from a specific individual, gathering social information through iterated predictions, and removing outliers.

Vetr is an example of an investor platform that makes use of social information by providing crowdsourced stock ratings for stocks and exchange-traded funds. On Vetr, users can search for specific stocks, review ratings from other investors who have shared insights on stocks they are interested in, add stocks to their watch-list, and trade stocks on that information. "The system we have designed is not about timing the market, rather it's about helping investors make better investment decisions," explained Vetr CEO Mike Vien. Vetr users make specific predictions about the future price of a particular stock. Users who do especially well at beating the market are rewarded through social recognition and their reputations are promoted on the site as a "Top Rater".

Vetr's algorithms then calculate a crowd target price and an aggregate rating from the users' target price predictions for the stock as well as users' past performance history. Traditionally, top raters have come from a variety of backgrounds, but Vetr's "theory is that when you have a broad distribution of people, coupled with diversity and independence, the predictions are better than industry experts", Vien says. "Our research demonstrates that Vetr's aggregated predictions are more informative about future stock prices than any individual Wall Street analyst or the target price consensus of industry professionals only[25]."

Today, it is perhaps best to view prediction markets as an application of predictive analytics to markets. Predictive analytics can have far wider applications than markets. Customer analytics, for example, is an extremely lucrative field of application. For instance, Framed Data started as a platform for data scientists to run and test markets before evolving to use machine learning technology to predict user churn and other customer metrics[26].

III. FROM CRISIS, OPPORTUNITY

A conversation with MIT Sloan Professor Andrew Lo explored the relationship between the global financial crisis of 2008 and recent evolutions of prediction markets[27]. The global financial crisis caused many people to lose confidence in the financial markets and some of the newer financial innovations. In many people's eyes prediction markets failed to live up to their promise. That confidence further decayed as centralized prediction markets, created to allow user predictions to be packed and traded as securities, were deemed gambling by US regulatory bodies, resulting in a number being shut down. Eight years after the financial crisis, the subsequent developments in prediction markets now offer a new promise that is reflective of some of the lessons learned from the crash.

Any deep innovation requires time and commitment to overcome skepticism. Prediction models face a number of skeptics who view them as weird and difficult to implement. As with many hyped trends, the future promise of the technology was not in line with the current abilities. The crisis and subsequent research has also offered a deeper understanding of the implicit assumptions and limitations of these models.

The New Machine Systems

So what's different now? First, technology developments can now more readily deliver the promise of prediction markets. Second, we have a better understanding about the human element underpinning these models.

Looking at the technology, we see developments in data availability, and that quantitative hedge funds have moved towards a purer model of machine learning. Not only have prediction methods reached speeds that enable high-speed action while analyzing ever larger amounts of data, a huge step forward has been made in how the algorithms learn. There are many different learning models used today, for example, neural networks that draw design inspiration from neurons in the human brain used independently or in concert. The results of these developments are that more data types, specifically raw live-feed data from real-world systems, can be analyzed without having to be preprocessed by hand, and consequently real-time analysis methods allow trading strategies to adapt to live market data.

Hedge funds were some of the first financial adopters of predictions markets and are still experimenting with new ways to push the technology forward. One way is by uniting Artificial Intelligence (AI) with prediction markets.

In January of 2016, Aidyia officially launched its AI hedge fund, in which all trades are executed entirely by machine. Their system identifies and executes its own trading strategies entirely autonomously using multiple forms of AI, from one inspired by genetic evolution to another using probabilistic logic. Analyzing everything from prices to macroeconomic data and corporate accounting documents, the Aidyia AI makes its own market predictions and then uses a probabilistic assessment to make its decisions[27]. Another example is Sentient, a distributed artificial intelligence platform that has first been used for trading, which is now being extended to other areas such as e-commerce and healthcare. Sentient is based on two pillars - evolutionary intelligence and deep learning. Sentient Investment Management develops and applies proprietary quantitative trading and investment strategies, and Sentient Aware helps customers find products they want by using visual search[28].

Numerai is an example of a start-up that is combining crowdsourcing and AI. Numerai is a hedge fund which harnesses and aggregates promising machine learning models from the masses, in the form of a global artificial intelligence tournament to predict the stock market. Using advanced encryption techniques, Numerai is able to give access to very private data to amateur and veteran data scientists all over the world while still ensuring that those data are not spread further. Users operate very much like consultants, contributing their human capital, without putting up any financial capital of their own. Payment is made through blockchain currencies and all interfacing happens through a distributed network and in an anonymous manner[29].

One direction to take these technological advancements is to try remove the human element from the decision making process. In specific scenarios, this will be a potentially lucrative approach, but does not incorporate some of the other learnings from the crash.

The Challenges Limiting Prediction Markets

Any type of predictive analytics makes you a prisoner of the past. When creating and testing models you are always back testing against historical data. More and more evidence shows that markets are not only dynamic but adapting at pace much faster than previously seen. A few years ago, high frequency trading was measured in minutes, where now it's measured in fractions of a second. The financial crisis showed us data never before seen in the public US markets and it wreaked havoc on predictions. Machine learning can do correlation very well but the gap between correlation, a pattern, and causation, a driving cause, is a long distance. The only way to fill that gap is through the narrative and context given to those patterns. An example of this approach is Endor. com, cofounded by Prof. Pentland, which couples quantitative models of human behavior with more standard machine learning techniques. As a consequence, they are able to derive accurate predictions from much shorter time-series data than other systems, allowing quicker reactions in volatile situations. This is particularly useful for churn, fraud, and similar prediction tasks where losses can happen quite quickly.

The second big change for prediction markets is in understanding, enabling and incentivizing the human behaviors of prediction markets. First, even in the relatively short span of eight years we have collectively become more tech savvy and connected. Tapping into the wisdom of crowds can be an almost frictionless process when individuals are motivated to contribute.

The ability to add more people would seem to add more wisdom to the crowd, and thus offering more predictive power. However, this is not always true: independent observations are critical to the idea of wisdom of crowds, primarily because they offered a diversity of information. Consequently small but highly independent "crowds" can still have predictive power, while large but highly connected crowds may not have significant predictive power. Natural human behavioral biases arise when an individual is aware of other people's opinions. The running adage about the world getting smaller is true, particularly when you are talking about one asset type in one market in one industry, which calls into question the independence of the crowds' observations.

Beyond the Echo Chamber

Machines are not capable of making an intuitive leap, and humans are subject to mental biases - but what about human/machine systems? While most players are making a big push to advance machine learning technology, our team at MIT has sought to get a better understanding of social learning, to more clearly understand how people make decisions and follow idea flow through a human network. Published in the study "Beyond the Echo Chamber"[30], by looking at financial decision making among traders using a transparent and social trading platform, the study observed not only the ideal balance of information diversity and network connectivity that will enhance decision making skills, but more importantly that decision making skills could be improved through social learning.

Those that excelled at decision making are social explorers, continuously seeking out new people and ideas—but not using some preconceived notion about the "best" people or ideas. Social explorers seek connections with a diversity of people and to gain exposure to a large variety of viewpoints. The results of the analysis revealed that the effects of social learning were significantly better payoffs than peers. The traders who had the right balance and diversity of ideas in their network yielded 30% higher returns on investments than the returns of either isolated traders or those in the herd.

The research proved that if the flow of ideas becomes either too sparse or too dense, relatively small adjustments in a person's social learning strategy can help correct the situation. By providing small incentives or nudges to individuals, isolated traders could be encouraged to engage more while traders who are too interconnected within the same group could explore outside their immediate social network. With the help of deep learning techniques, this social network could be tuned so that it remained in the healthy "wisdom of the crowds" balance.

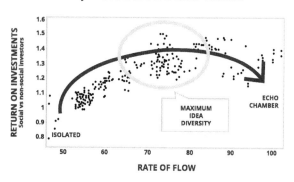

Utilizing these corrections in a large-scale experiment, the MIT team increased the return on investments of all social traders by more than 6%. Managing idea flows using the "idea flow" prediction model resulted in meaningful enhancements to human behaviors, also proving that markets can be structured with adaptive incentives to create better "wisdom of crowds" results. In this case it helped turn middling traders—often losers in the financial system—into winners[31].

IV. PREDICTING THE FUTURE OF PREDICTION MARKETS

Information asymmetry drives competitive edge in finance, so the most successful work is the least talked about. To better uncover some of the trends we talked with researchers both within universities and at companies working on the future generations of prediction markets. Focusing on better predictions as well as new avenues for growth are some of the key trends centered on new data and technologies and new application areas.

New Data and Technologies

In addition to continuing to evolve better machine learning models, the push for greater amounts of unique data is a big focus of innovators, coupled with the corresponding integration of this new data with machine learning, prediction markets, and other modeling technology. Data has become an increasingly important competitive advantage, and there is an ever greater push for faster and novel data.

Thomson Reuters, for instance, is responding to this sort of client demand by experimenting with new business models and data collection methods, partially through its newly created Thomson Reuters Lab. One method of developing such new business models and new data is to look for companies with a unique perspective on a market, such as a company with large operations in a niche market. Reuters can work with such a company to anonymize and monetize their data for Reuters's audience. For prediction markets, having diversified information that is not otherwise readily accessible opens up unique and profitable opportunities.

Speaking with Henry Chong from Thomson Reuters Labs, he predicts the business of information is poised to change as new prediction technologies enter the market. Human data or data tied to physical content, collecting new forms and understanding it will play a greater role in the future.

We have seen AI and prediction markets converge, and the future could see further exploration with other emerging technologies such as blockchain and IoT. One such project, Augur, is exploring the union of two of these by creating a blockchain-based prediction market. Built upon the Truthcoin protocol, the goal is to prove prediction markets can be leveraged for social good by using a decentralized public ledger as a mechanism for fields such as healthcare and government to tap into the predictive power of global users. For example, if you wanted to research foods that can cause cancer, the sheer volume of information is overwhelming, as is the prospect of slogging through the amount of conflicting, misleading or pseudo-scientific work that exists. With a searchable prediction market using incentivized participants, you could find an opinion based on the wisdom of crowds rather than reviewing individual studies from lone experts[32,33].

New Application Areas

Prediction markets are not just limited to finance or political polling. Used in other areas such as baseball – Rebellion Research for example uses learning networks to predict specific trade outcomes as well as market trends – the prediction market industry will continue to grow. But it's not just external, but rather internal company markets that are most promising. Forecasting for internal outcomes such as supply and demand imbalances is one example, which has proven previously successful. Not an entirely novel use, HP previously created an internal prediction market to forecast printer sales, which proved more accurate than their traditional marketing forecasting models. At Siemens, an internal market accurately predicted that a new software product would fail to be delivered on time, even though all the project planning tools projected that the deadlines would be met. In each case these were small "crowds" of 20 and 60 employees respectively[34]. This highlights the criticality of participants providing unique information to help draw a more complete future picture. Set up properly, companies can use prediction markets to leverage the knowledge of employees, knowledge that is often invisible to more senior management, in order to enable better decision making.

Further development and deployment of human/machine prediction systems will be another powerful future direction as well. This entails creating machine learning networks that will enable and enhance, rather than replace, human decision making. Part of this new human-machine approach will be using AI to embed proper structure and incentives into prediction markets by augmenting human abilities, building AI models that can automatically implement adaptive incentive structures to correct for negative human behaviors.

CHAPTER 6

Digital Banking Manifesto

Alex Lipton, David Shrier, Alex Pentland

I. INTRODUCTION

"Banks are trying to be cool and hip and build super cool digital front ends... But it's like putting lipstick on a pig - ultimately it's still a pig and the new front end is still running into an awful digital back end."

- Mark Mullen, Chief Executive, Atom, Durham UK

We are entering a new era of innovation that will reshape consumers' relationships with their banks. In order to understand how banking will evolve in the digital age, it is important to understand its basic premise. While reasonable people can disagree about nuances, at heart, the art of banking is one of skillful record keeping in the double-entry general ledger. At micro level, banks can be thought of as dividend producing machines seeking deposits and issuing loans. At macro level, they are creators of credit money.[1] The main determinants of their quality and reliability are the amount of capital and the level of liquidity (essentially central bank money) they keep. In general, a bank would like to maintain the right levels of both – if it has too little, it becomes fragile, if it has too much, it becomes unprofitable and hence unable to fulfill its purpose of paying dividends. Some of the loans issued by the bank will be repaid as expected, and some will default. In general, when loans are repaid, the bank's capital grows and when they default, the capital diminishes. If the bank's capital falls below a certain fraction of its risk-weighted assets, the bank defaults. Good bankers differ from bad ones by their ability to attract a large pool of reliable borrowers, so that default levels stay close to their expected values. (Some defaults are inevitable and are accounted for by charging interest.) At the same time, good bankers need to attract long-term depositors and serve them well, so that depositors do not suddenly withdraw their deposits. If the latter were to happen, the bank can exhaust its liquid reserves and default through a different route. In principle, if its less liquid assets are sound, the central bank, which is called the lender of last resort for a reason, can come to the rescue and provide additional liquidity.

It is clear from the above description that banking activity is mostly technological and mathematical in nature. Hence, it is well suited to be digitized, yet the prevalence of legacy systems and legacy culture inhibits banks from embracing innovation as much as they should in order to survive and thrive in the digital economy of the 21 century. The root causes of banking malaise should be obvious – old-fashioned banks are far behind the latest technological breakthroughs; they also have a poor handle of the risks on their books. While major industries, including retail, travel, communications, and mass media have undergone revolutionary changes in their business models in the last thirty years or so, banking remained static at its core, living on its past glories and ignoring the winds of changes. Existing banks suffer from numerous drawbacks, because competition among them is relatively weak. Moreover, their customers are generally not happy with the level of customer service they receive, besides, they are exposed to the risk of losing their deposits (above and beyond the regulatory guaranteed minimum) in the case of their bank's default. Zero or negative deposit rates, which became prevalent in most developed countries in recent years, make keeping money in the bank both risky and unprofitable. Yet, at present, customers do not have viable alternatives.

In addition, there are whole strata of people and SME, especially in developing countries, who are either underbanked or unbanked, due to the fact that traditional banking methods are not flexible enough either to solve the know your customer (KYC) problem for them or to assess their credit worthiness.

Thanks to new developments in data technology and in mobile telecommunications adoption, we see the potential rise of a third wave of innovation in banking. We will outline in this chapter the key features, benefits, and strategic imperative of the Digital Bank of the Future (DBF).

To understand the opportunity that is promulgating this third wave, we define the first two waves of digital innovation in banking:

FIRST WAVE COMPANIES: THE "INCREMENTALISTS"

Digital technologies have been entering the banking industry for years. However, they have been added incrementally to existing operations, either as an overlay or a minor extension. We term these the "incrementalists" or First Wave companies.

In the mid 1970s, Citi began experimenting with the automated teller machine (ATM). Former MIT Chairman John Reed led the development of Citi's efforts in this area, revolutionizing retail banking. The ATM story is a landmark study in corporate innovation. The concept was simple: deploy machines that could process transactions such as cash withdrawals and check deposits. What was revolutionary was what followed: banks historically had been open with limited daytime hours, say 9am – 3pm, which was inconvenient for people who had a job. However, in the 1950's, most householders in the U.S. had a single earner, and the stay-at-home-wife was able to handle banking needs during the day. Mapping to a behavior change in society, as more and more women entered the workforce, the U.S. saw a rise in two-income households, which in turn led to a diminution in the ability of people to take advantage of daytime banking services. Thanks to computerized banking, executives could see exactly when people most needed to use banking services. Evening utilization of ATMs surged. Banks, in turn, then began extending their hours into the evening to accommodate the working professional. By 2014, there were 524,000 tellers in the U.S.[2], up from 484,000 in 1985[3].

Online banking, likewise, was piloted in the 1980s by Citi, Chemical Bank, through Minitel (France), and Prestel (UK), but didn't really take off until the 1990s in conjunction with soaring internet usage. Simple, browser-based tools gave consumers access to a number of key banking transactions such as money transfer, bank statements, and electronic bill payment. While the incumbent commercial banks initially were the purveyors of online banking, the rise of the internet also saw the rise of the internet bank – most prominently NetBank in 1996.

SECOND WAVE COMPANIES: DIGITAL HYBRIDS

We term the Second Wave companies like NetBank to be "Digital Hybrids". Frequently taking advantage of front end systems to better market and connect with consumers, they remain shackled by legacy back and middle office infrastructure, risk modeling systems, and sometimes labor models. Often these hybrid banks will have an incumbent bank as their backend.

For example, Simple Bank was founded in 2009 with a number of innovations to streamline account management and costs, but uses The Bancorp as its backend.

Other emergent hybrid banks such as Fidor Bank (Germany), Atom Bank (UK), LHV Pank (Estonia), and DBS Digibank (Singapore) enjoy purpose-built IT infrastructure that is 60-80% less expensive to build, and 30-50% less expensive to maintain, than legacy banks. Headcount is considerably lower, about 10-15% the levels of a traditional bank.

However, these "digital hybrids" still use centralized databases, cloud based storage and primitive user data protocols. They represent a bridge solution between the Main Street bank of yesterday and the fully digital bank of the future.

THIRD WAVE COMPANIES: DIGITAL NATIVES

A new set of technologies is emerging that permit close integration with consumers' lives, promise access to the 2.5 billion unbanked or underbanked consumers globally[4], and greater financial flexibility to 45+ million underbanked Small & Medium-sized Enterprises (SMEs) around the world[5].

DBF will take advantage of these technologies and be designed around the needs of digital natives, the 50 and under crowd that grew up with computers as a daily part of their lives. For the millennials, a mobile-first strategy will drive ease of access and rapid adoption through seamless integration with their lives.

Taking a breakthrough approach to data security, DBF will eschew a central data repository, easily attacked, in favor of a secure, encrypted, distributed data system. Personal data stores not only permit better digital walleting, but also greater security around personal biometric data which is integral to the digital bank's security protocols.

The new technology paradigm begs the question: what role do banks truly have in the new world? Have we reached the end of banks in the way we know them? Is it possible that fractional banking is on its last legs and the introduction of government issued digital cash which can be stored in a digital wallet outside the banking system will put the last nail in its coffin?

We will now look at the key requirements for a digital bank from three perspectives: customer, investor, and the bank itself.

II. KEY REQUIREMENTS FOR A DIGITAL BANK – CUSTOMERS' PERSPECTIVE

Consumer View of Future Digital Bank

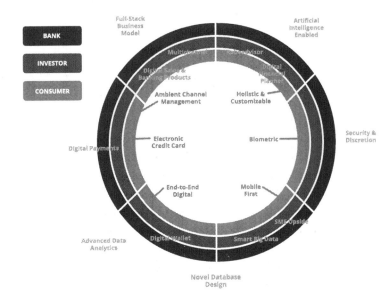

At a minimum, on the retail side, DBF should be able to do the following:

- **Holistic & Customizable Experience** Provide a holistic, interactive, and intuitive overview of the customers' money and, more broadly, their financial life, including information on their current account and deposit balances, transactions, outstanding loans, recurring payments, pension contributions and accumulation as well as securities accounts. Tailor its services for different customer segments such as small and informal merchants, mass affluent, youth market, international travelers, or low-income customers. Offer a trusted and relatively inexpensive source of credit for its customers;

- **End-to-End Digital** Provide a holistic fully digital experience for customers, including, paperless application and passing of the KYC (Know Your Client) process. Also provide an interactive and intuitive digital financial planner to organize customers' financial life and optimize their resources: immediate cash flow requirements, savings, including tools for automatic savings, medical expenses, education, retirement, including robo-advisory with services previously accessible by high end investors only, investments, including tools for trading securities. Empower customers to electronically apply for mortgage or loan, competitive insurance contracts for home, liability, medical and travel insurance, with credit checking procedures expanded to social media. Provide reporting documentation related to bank activity, including tax statements, etc. Provide access to Personal Data Store (PDS);

- **Mobile First** Enable natively driven mobile e-payment solutions, including domestic and international payments and remittances, automatic bill payments, and peer-to-peer (P2P) payments and money transfers. Rather than having mobile as an afterthought or an added capability, everything changes if you start with mobile and build out from there – not just UX but fundamental infrastructure and credit analytics;

- **Foreign Exchange** Deliver seamless and inexpensive foreign exchange services, including protection against exchange rate fluctuations by providing multi-currency accounts. Potentially, a full range of instruments for hedging against foreign exchange risk, including forward contracts, spot contracts, swaps, and exchange traded options can be offered;

- **Biometrics** Offer biometric technology such as face and voice biometrics, already actively used at airports and international border controls, as core credentials for customers with preference for biometrics to PIN or password as a way of authentication for logging in. Behavioral biometric, which is being developed at the moment, is a promising venue for achieving an extra degree of protection;

- **E-Credit Card** Implement bank e-credit card based on customer's own preferences with pre-set limits and permitted transactions, consumption-related patterns, and a comprehensive digital wallet and PDS, which includes, at the minimum, electronic ID, e-card for secure online purchases, and tools to view, pay, organize, analyze, archive e-bills, and generate relevant tax documents;

- **Access to P2P World** Provide access to "crowd-everything" including P2P payment and lending opportunities.

III. KEY REQUIREMENTS FOR A DIGITAL BANK –
INVESTOR PERSPECTIVE

Investor View of Future Digital Bank

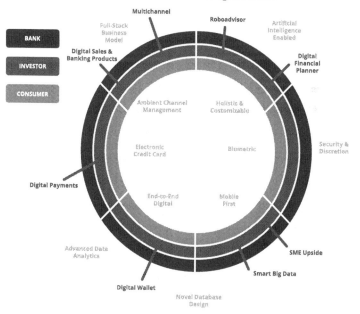

Digital bank is an exciting investment opportunity and inevitable business step because legacy banks are no longer able to adequately service their customers' needs in the digital age. Customer requirements simply cannot be met by traditional banks unable to catch up with the digital revolution. With neither real estate overhead, nor massive maintenance spending on legacy IT systems, digital banks expect to grow multibillion dollar balance sheets in several years of operations with the fraction of full time staff compared to traditional banks. For instance, Atom Bank in the UK intends to grow into a £5 billion balance sheet business in five years with just 340 full time staff, while legacy bank Metro has that size balance sheet with 2,200 people. It is clear, however, that the majority of digital banks' staff will be engineers and data scientists, although, as always, the role of sales and marketing should not be underestimated.

MONETIZATION AND CAPTURING VALUE

Compared to legacy banks, digital banks can generate value in numerous ways:

- **Digital Payments** Digital payments form the core of monetization. They include mobile and online payments, both domestic and foreign, as well as mobile P2P interactions. Digital payments enable banks to boost fees and interest income and reach a broader set of customers with more diverse services; they are done more cost effectively than by incumbent banks, allowing market share gains through competitive pricing and/or accessing 2.5bn unbanked & underbanked;

- **Digital wallet** Digital wallet is essential for digital commerce and ecosystems built on value-added services. In addition, it optimizes transaction costs for customers and funding costs for banking operations;

- **Digital Sales & Banking Products** Artificial intelligence (AI) assisted sales of banking products, such as deposits, loans, and mortgages are conducted through direct channels, including social media. That is in line with shifting consumer preferences and behavior trends in e-commerce, especially directed at Generation Y and tech-savvy customers;

- **Multichanneling** An integrated and seamless multichannel approach to sales increases the bank's share of customers' wallet, boosts customer loyalty, thereby making a significant difference in customer adoption rates;

- **Digital Financial Planner & Roboadvisory** AI-based digital financial planner manages monthly income, recurring payments, savings and investments, increasing interaction between the digital bank and customers. The bank acts as a trusted shepherd defining customer life-cycle financial needs. Logical continuation of the circle of trust between the digital bank and customers, where customers rely on the Roboadvisory services to optimize investment portfolios based on individual goals and preferences, regularly adjust them and record incremental results and properly allocate resources for each phase of the customer's voyage towards all things digital;

- **Smart Big Data** Advanced analytics allows the digital bank to transform its data into more personalized client service aimed at data monetization;

- **SME Upside** AI- and big-data based credit models enabling risk-managed provisioning of credit access to SMEs, banking the 45 million underbanked SMEs globally. By 2018, banks in Scandinavia, the United Kingdom, and Western Europe are forecast to have half or more of new inflow revenue coming from digital related activities in most products, such as savings and term deposits, and bank services to SMEs[6].

IV. KEY REQUIREMENTS FOR A DIGITAL BANK –
BANK'S PERSPECTIVE

"Banks are mired in the legacy of old IT systems that are bad... The first automated banking system was introduced by Coutts in 1967. The joke is that they are still running on it today." The only saving grace is that banks are not unique in this respect. For instance, as was revealed by a recent government report, the US nuclear weapons force still relies on a 1970s-era computer system and 8-inch floppy disks.

Bank's View of Future Digital Bank

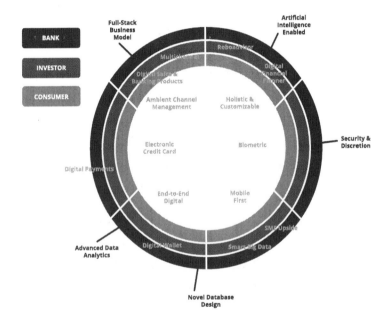

By its very nature, a digital bank has to be a cross between a Fintech company and a bank. While a digital bank, similarly to a conventional one, can be organized into five divisions: Retail Banking, Private and Business

Banking, Analytics and IT, Finance Management and Operations, and Risk Management, the relative importance of these departments is not the same. Moreover, the relationship map between various divisions is different in digital and legacy banking, with analytics and IT being the cornerstone of the digital banking edifice. In general, success and failure of a bank is measurable by technologies and analytical methods adopted rather than by its product line.

- **Novel IT Infrastructure** Building a digital bank from scratch enables to create a flexible IT infrastructure, which provides state of the art risk management, helps to optimize the bank's balance sheet to achieve return on capital significantly higher than return of the incumbents, and guarantees compliance with constantly changing banking regulations in real time, which is achieved via building modern RegTech capabilities.

- **Database Design** The bank IT is based on the state-of-the-art database technology, which can cope with the exponential growth in data, new internet technologies and analysis methods. This technology is expected to be based on distributed ledger framework.

- **Advanced Data Analytics** Since banks own rich reserves of raw behavioral data, which can provide valuable insights into future customer choices, the value proposition offered by digital banking can be extended. Following the example of Internet powerhouses, such as Google, Amazon, Alibaba, and Facebook, the bank should consolidate data across deposits, consumer finance, and other transaction accounts for a unified view of customer activities. For instance, customers' in-store payments are far more accurate than conventional profile data (for example, age, income, geography) in predicting their future financial activities and credit worthiness; their geospatial mobility among stores providing extra improvements.

In addition, using customer data, digital banks can create offerings ranging from payment solutions and information services, savings and deposit-taking right through to online banking, advisory services, and simple financing. It is imperative to be able to evaluate collected customer transactions in real time and connect them for prediction of future customer behavior using deep learning and other probabilistic algorithms. It is important to build in safeguards of customer privacy in accordance with their preferences and legal requirements.

- **Artificial Intelligence** Autonomous selection of best methodology when presented with arbitrary data enables banks to dynamically adopt to novel information and build a full financial profile of its customers, including credit worthiness, debt capacity, and risk appetite for financial planning. In addition, AI can rapidly adapt to customer needs and present the best offers at the right time, changing dynamically as the customer evolves. A "smart bank" can more rapidly capitalize on shifts in a customer's life cycle and assist them in achieving their financial goals.

- **Full-Stack Business Model** The full-stack business model is crucial to the total client experience. This approach facilitates the bank's compliance with the regulatory framework, which enforces money laundering and fraud prevention and guarantees customers' protection. In general, intelligent fraud detection and remediation systems can function in a far more superior fashion than conventional methods.

- **Security and Discretion** If implemented correctly, bulletproof security and customer protection is the area of a great competitive advantage for digital banks compared to other financial service providers. These features are embedded in a secure IT architecture from the onset and preclude both data misuse and data sales to third parties. They naturally include implementation of new cryptographically secured distributed data management [7].

V. DIGITAL CUSTOMER SEGMENT

Digital banks have several natural constituencies in both developed and, especially, developing economies [8]:

- Professional consumers with at least an undergraduate college education;

- Digitally educated middle upper-mass and mass-affluent professional and managerial consumers;

- Digitally savvy Gen Y (students and young professionals in their 20s to 30s) digital-banking natives, who are exceedingly digitally savvy. They will form the foundation of the customer base for the digital bank;

- SMEs that go mainstream using a digital banking platform designed for their needs; potentially banking 45 million underbanked or unbanked SMEs globally [9].

VI. UNLEASHING DIGITAL CURRENCY

Digital banking of the future is unimaginable without using digital currency [10]. Currently, both central and private banks are actively pursuing creation of digital currencies. Some considerations for this dimension:

- **Non-Bank Digital Currencies** While the best known digital currency is Bitcoin, it's not suited for high volume transactions because of its low transactions per second (TPS) capacity. It is likely that other digital currencies based on consensus achievable by means other than proof-of-work will be used in digital banking. One should not forget that Bitcoin is not the first digital currency to emerge, nor is it going to be the last. In fact, it is possible that digital cash invented by David Chaum more than thirty years ago can see a comeback at the next level of efficiency.

- **Central Bank Digital Currencies** Several central banks are investigating whether a state-backed digital currency could reduce capital outflow, money laundering and tax evasion, and make economic activity more transparent and efficient. For instance, PBOC, BoE and Bank of Russia are all actively looking in this direction. In this scenario, the "free" (or very inexpensive) deposits that commercial banks have been benefiting from will evaporate.

- **Private Bank Digital Currencies** The idea of banks issuing their own currency is very old. For instance, dozens of banks in the United States were doing so in the nineteenth century. Advances in digitization made this idea viable again. For example, Bank of Tokyo Mitsubishi UFJ (MUFJ) is developing its own digital currency, MUFG coin, and the corresponding smartphone application prototype to authenticate digital tokens on a P2P platform. The bank expects to rein in financial transactional costs, including cheaper international remittance and money transfers. Moreover, in the future the bank might potentially issue its digital currency to customers.[11]

- **Distributed Ledger** Using distributed ledger reduces financial transaction costs, improves resilience of the system as a whole, and mitigates operational risks. Without doubt, distributed ledger will become intertwined with operational procedures of a digital bank and its interactions with other digital, legacy and central banks.

VII. ECOSYSTEM

It is natural to expect that a well-designed digital bank will become the corner stone of a much bigger financial ecosystem. As important constituent parts of such an ecosystem, one can think of such digital service providers as insurers, brokers, wealth managers, robo-advisors, credit card issuers, cross-border payment providers, currency exchanges, P2P lenders, etc. The ability of these companies to satisfy the financial needs of their clients will be greatly enhanced by their access to a wider financial system through the digital bank. At the same, the bank will benefit by getting additional information about their customers' demands and habits, thus closing the information feedback loop [12]. Moreover, digital cash issued by the bank can serve as a lubricant allowing the wheels of commerce to spin faster and much more efficiently than is currently possible.

We envision a digital bank of the future in the center of the internet of things (IoT), which can be thought of as the bank of things (BoT). For instance, if a bank's client house informs him or her that the roof needs repairs, the bank can immediately recommend several contractors, organize bids, help the client to choose the most suitable one, and arrange financing. Thus, in addition to financial businesses, a digital bank of the future can incorporate into its ecosystem various non-financial actors. All these developments will enhance social utility of the bank and its appreciation by the public while, at the same time, increasing its profitability. Banks have to keep in mind that there is no time to lose, because the competition for their customers' digital wallet from current digital champions, such as Google, Amazon, Facebook and Alibaba, will be fierce.

VIII. BEYOND BANKS

The unsatisfactory state of affairs with existing banks opens a unique opportunity for building a digital bank from scratch. Such a bank will fulfill its mission by utilizing the most advanced technologies, including cryptography and distributed ledger techniques, artificial intelligence, big data, and deep learning. From the very beginning, it will be based on balance sheet optimization, deployment of digital distributed ledger-inspired infrastructure, and comprehensive automation and digitization of the middle and back office, as well as a heightened security employing the most advanced cryptographic techniques throughout the entire organization. By design, this bank will be highly efficient, profitable and agile. In addition, its infrastructure will be flexible enough to handle both private digital currencies (such as Bitcoin) and potential government issued currencies (such as Britcoin). If so desired, this bank will be capable of issuing its own digital currency. The bank will liberally apply artificial intelligence and big data analytics for creating unparalleled customer experience, automating personal and SME credit issuance, and improving risk management. By design, such a bank will be valued by investors, customers, and regulators alike.

And yet, by building a bank, are we trapped in the old paradigm?

If you look at WeChat or Sesame, you will see what is scaring the C-level of even leading edge companies like Facebook and Google, to say nothing of the fright induced at leading telecommunications companies. Perhaps surprisingly, many legacy banks seem to be more sanguine. WeChat is redefining what financial services means in relation to the broader suite of consumer services individuals engage with.

The key is having customer-centric data across all areas of life, held in standard format with standard APIs that work across all the entire digital ecosystem and not just its financial services or products corner (like a universal Personal Data Store, but customers don't own or manage it; they do). Using this central, panoptic data, WeChat can integrate services from the whole range of life opportunities (entertainment, work, finance, family, etc.) in a seamless and consistent manner.

What this gives customers is fully integrated payments, credit and banking, unbelievable advising capability and amazing KYC and AML, all in a form that is completely transparent. Consumers don't need to know that payments are different from credit or from banking or from shopping in general. Users just wander around online and in-person, finding interesting things and buy, sell and trade seamlessly. WeChat or Sesame is also integrating health, lifestyle and employment services with money services - completely transparently; no separate apps of web pages. You can just take care of what you need to live a better life. However, this is conditional on consumers' ability to secure credit as necessary. Given the rather uncertain and limited capacity of P2P networks to provide credit, digital banks have to come to the rescue.

A similar future is unfolding for SMEs: customers are shepherded to buy and money flow issues like credit, payments, KYC and AML go away virtually completely. WeChat reportedly reached over one million SMEs integrated into their services in the first few months of operations.

Is there a future that is NO banking versus "digital banking"? Instead, banking functions are just integrated invisibly everywhere. Several immediate challenges come to mind with this model:

- Due to the special and unique role of banks in credit money creation, non-bank actors simply do not have necessary capacity to satisfy the financial needs of their customers;

- There are numerous constraints around offering banking services that may be too limiting for companies in western Europe and the US. If China begins to adopt more restrictive financial regulations to better protect consumers, they too will create a less hospitable business environment for these kinds of services.

- Will WeChat (or the next WeChat) want to take its high flying tech company stock market multiple, and burden it with a financial services discount [13]? The more successful it gets at financial services, the more acute this question becomes. However, if financialization of a tech company is done in a deliberate and measured way, it can actually increase the shareholder value.

Despite these challenges, is there a model that we could call "invisible banking" that integrates into our daily lives without friction? The answer is yes and no – the legacy banking model will unquestionably disappear over time, but in the transition period, digital banks will have a role in daily life for the foreseeable future as transaction lubricants and enablers.

CHAPTER 7

Policy & Fintech:

How Regulators Think about Financial Innovation
And How Financial Innovators Think about Regulation

Oliver Goodenough, David Shrier,
Thomas Hardjono, Alex Pentland

I. INTRODUCTION: FINANCIAL INNOVATION AND REGULATORY CONCERNS

Technology has driven innovative changes in many areas of human activity over the past half century, and the financial industry has been no exception. Advances such as the SWIFT system, electronic trading systems, and automated settlement were revolutionary a generation or two ago; now they are business as usual. Aside from the movement towards arms-length trading fueled by advances in derivatives and securitization, however, the overall structure of the financial system hasn't changed that dramatically. In this way, finance is following a pattern of development common in many industries.

We are moving from a model of technology empowering human players within the current system, to one that replaces many of the human players within the current system, to (inevitably) one where technology overturns much of the current system and replaces it with something else[1]. Much of the innovation already digested in the financial system falls into the first two categories. The thesis we outline in this book is that, we are facing developments in finance that begin to look like the third category: something with new and not fully anticipatable outcomes. A series of developments such as blockchain, mobile money, smart instruments, big data, predictive markets, and secure identity are part of the possible revolution.

Among the many uncertainties that are raised by this vision of disruptive change, regulatory concerns have a significant role. As anyone active in the field knows, the financial system operates within a highly developed set of government rules that can be thought of as the "regulatory framework." Rules apply to the markets and the transactions within them, to the institutions and to their governance, their operations and their net worth, to the nature of currencies and to the use of data. The list goes on and on. Trying to anticipate the shape of regulatory response, whether prohibitive or enabling, is a key factor in trying to formulate strategies for playing in the world that may be dawning.

This chapter will provide both background and some use-case examples for better approaching this task of anticipation. Against this background, we will explore some of the fundamental policy, regulatory, and governance issues confronting blockchain and related innovations in finance[2]. For the purposes of this chapter, we use the term "regulation" and its variations to encompass a broad range of legal rules, including those made by statute and court decisions as well as those made by regulatory agencies[3].

We argue that, as with any sociotechnical system, blockchain and other disruptive technologies will typically require formal governance mechanisms — including laws and regulations — to achieve their full potential. The details of these mechanisms should vary, depending on the specific use case under consideration. For example, a digital currency for retail-scale payments will have different needs from a registration system for land titles.

We suggest that regulation has an important, and even helpful, role to play in fostering the adoption of blockchain and other financial technologies.

It is easy to see, for instance, how laws requiring everyone to drive on the same side of the road can speed travel and improve road safety, how standardized weights and measures can facilitate gains to specialization in manufacturing, or how regulations forbidding Ponzi schemes can reduce overall borrowing costs by attracting investors to the market. In contrast to these established examples of productive intervention to solve coordination problems and market failures, the blockchain and related technologies are still in their early days. Predicting where their pain points will be most severe or where their successes will be most transformative is necessarily a speculative enterprise.

The discussion that follows is intentionally illustrative rather than exhaustive. We want to show the diversity of challenges that arise in engineering technologically based innovations in our financial system, as well as to provide a frame of reference for thinking about those examples. The catalog of possibilities is meant as a starting point. We hope to inspire critical thinking about the issues and approaches to developing blockchain technology, and to encourage the stakeholders (government officials, entrepreneurs, ethicists, community activists , developers, others) to pursue a reasoned approach to regulation.

II. REGULATORY GOALS AND TECHNIQUES

1. WHY DO WE REGULATE?

This section focuses first on why and how regulation happens, highlighting some key guiding principles. It will then explore some of the players in the existing regulatory structure that governs the financial system. In later sections we will apply these principles to the blockchain and other financial innovations. The topic of regulatory design is not a settled one; there are significant arguments and disagreements over where, what and how regulatory approaches should be applied[4]. That said, there are also some generally recognized guidelines that cut across the debates[5]. The summary provided here represents a synthesis by the authors in their private capacities, rather than a definitive treatment with governmental authority, and should be viewed in that light.

Maximizing the benefits and minimizing the detriments of an advance like the blockchain is not simply a matter of technology. As the economist Paul Romer notes[6]:

> "Economic growth is driven by the coevolution of two sets of ideas, technologies and rules. Governments can increase the rate of growth—in ways that benefit all citizens—by creating systems of rules that are both encouraging of and response to innovation; the various goals do not always line up."

To the economist's goal of efficiency, we should properly add the lawyer's additional criteria of fairness, justice and sustainability.

2. JURISDICTION

There is a diversity of possible sources of authority in the *making* of rules and also in *applying* them to a particular activity. Who gets to do what is often framed as a question of "jurisdiction." What is criminal in one country may be perfectly acceptable in another. Some countries exert *extraterritorial jurisdiction* for some activities, such as the criminal treatment of genocide, but this is relatively rare. More usual is the case when a country is sufficiently concerned about the *effects* of an activity within its borders to assert jurisdiction even if the primary event takes place somewhere outside. Particularly in markets like the financial markets, where money flows across borders and often to the places of highest yield or safest harbor, countries often affirmatively coordinate common standards of conduct to avoid creating arbitrage opportunities or unfair advantage for one jurisdiction over another. For instance, fraudulent offers are commonly outlawed regardless of the country of origin.

A further wrinkle on jurisdiction is the ability of the authority in question to get physical control over the person, asset, or other item that is the target of the regulation. This is particularly challenging in the case of cyber activities, where, for instance, the effects may be felt in the United States, but where all of the players are in another region of the globe. There are possibilities for attempting to extend the legal reach of a country, such as extradition, blocking web access, or the freezing of local accounts, but these often have only limited effect.

Blockchain enabled activities present particularly interesting jurisdictional challenges because of their inherently dispersed and virtual character. The decentralized and sometimes anonymous nature of blockchain-based transactions is unlikely to remove them from the power of governmental oversight, notwithstanding the claims of the more libertarian end of the technology spectrum. The Internet has posed similar questions, and governments have asserted authority in a wide swath of contexts. Enforcement of government authority over a dispersed worldwide activity may be a challenge, but as the travails of Silk

Road demonstrate, a determined government can overwhelm someone it views as a serious criminal[7].

3. REGULATORY GOALS

What are the proper goals for regulation? Some are cast in negative terms: to prevent harm, both intentional and accidental, whether direct or incidental. Preventing outright predation is usually easy to justify. Innovation, on the other hand, typically harms incumbent interests, and judging when to let such harm proceed is more difficult to assess. The Luddites of 18th century Britain are often mocked for their opposition to progress, but the negative *local* implications of innovation for wealth and job security may be quite severe (e.g., when the plant closes in a company town), even if the innovation is raising productivity in the aggregate. Similar forces have been cited as underlying electoral discontent, as revealed in the U.K.'s Brexit vote, and the popularity of "outsider" Bernie Sanders and Donald Trump in the U.S.

Some goals are more positive: to provide an institutional framework within which an activity can grow productively. Others are in the selfish interest of government itself, whether to raise revenue or to consolidate power over an activity. These interests can be perfectly legitimate, even when they impose a drag on the activity itself. Less justifiable are examples of "regulatory capture," where private interests use the power of government to entrench their position in an economic activity. Further complicating the regulatory response to innovation, the various goals do not always line up. Careful regulatory policy often involves the balancing of competing goods and competing harms, so that both the utopian hopes of the innovator and the catastrophic fears of the traditionalist are seldom fully realized.

THE CLINTON/MAGAZINER ECOMMERCE PRINCIPLES

The Clinton/Magaziner eCommerce principles, helped provide a foundation for successful commercial development of internet eCommerce in the U.S. Without sacrificing the public good, they are instructive for considering how to regulate other fintech innovations, like blockchain[8]. Briefly, the principles provide for:

- Maximize possibility of human freedom since the medium holds great potential to support individual liberty.
- Expressly allow voluntary communities to form.
- Where possible, the rules should be set by private, nonprofit, stakeholder-based groups (such as Internet Engineering Task Force or the W3C Consortium).
- Government action should occur sparingly, transparently, in a targeted manner, and via a common agreement that action is needed.
- Respect that internet eCommerce is a decentralized, fast-moving medium, and foster policies that are neutral to specific technologies.
- By its very nature, it is global, and therefore an international framework is needed from the outset (rather than the legacy systems where markets evolve locally, and then governments coordinate with each other as internationalization occurs).

Preventing Harm. The easiest case for legal intervention involves rules against intentional predation – e.g. physical attack, theft, fraud, and deceit. For example, Bernie Madoff was jailed for willfully defrauding his investors. Also objectionable is reckless behavior, where the harm *per se* is not intentional, but where any consideration for the prevention of harm is lacking. The failure of underwriters to scrutinize poorly documented subprime mortgages adequately at the point of origination could fall into this category. A third category is harm arising through accidents or unintended systemic effects. A classic example is the bank run, in which the infectious panic of nervous depositors can force even a healthy bank into default.

To justify regulation, a harm need not be inherent in an activity itself, if it is frequently a means to carry out some other harmful action. For instance, a concern often voiced over virtual currencies is that they facilitate illicit trafficking in drugs, arms and people.

Providing an Institutional Framework for Private Creativity. Commercial law provides institutional scaffolding for the design and enforcement of *private* bargains. Contract law is a prime example. At its best, contract law creates a toolkit for designing the enforceable obligations that make specialization and exchange possible, and open up possibilities for mutual gain. By making bargains enforceable in *law*, they become much more reliable, and a number of strategic pitfalls can be avoided. On the other hand, contracting between parties with too much disparity in experience or power has risks for deception and predation as well. A good contract framework will discourage fraud by stipulating requirements for disclosure and boundaries of unconscionability[9]. Thus, an appropriate legal scaffolding will *promote* the activity it regulates by solving trust problems that might otherwise hinder adoption. Government intervention to encourage *confidence* in a process is a buttress, not a burden. A familiar example is the oversight of our stock exchanges, where private rules receive public scrutiny under the Securities Exchange Act of 1934.

Much of the interest in blockchain technologies is that they can help solve these sorts of trust dilemmas. The technology, however, involves relatively arcane cryptographic techniques. A legal framework that helps create confidence that a particular blockchain is properly administered could foster adoption.

ENABLING RULES AND JURISDICTIONAL COMPETITION

Each of the technology-based financial innovations discussed in this book raises questions about the current and future adequacy of the legal and regulatory framework to allow its adoption, support its utility, govern its conduct, and resolve disputes.

Adoption of blockchain and other financial technologies will benefit from adaptations in the code and regulation to foster its growth and adoption. For example, state legislatures[10] and national regulators (Bank of Japan) are considering new rules to ensure legal recognition for blockchain technology (for a wide range of recorded materials in Vermont and currency in Japan). While Japan has said it has "no specific scheme in place," it is watching developments closely and actively discussing the technology[11].

The failure of a jurisdiction to supply the supporting regulatory or legal framework could encourage the migration of blockchain-based services away from the traditional financial sector and the purview of existing supervisors. Jurisdictions such as Barbados have explicitly positioned themselves as fintech havens[12]. There is a long history of jurisdiction-shopping by ambitious entrepreneurs, often matched by a "competition in laxity"[13] among eager regulators. The challenge, of course, is to prevent support for innovation from devolving into thoughtless permissiveness.

Raising Public Revenue. Governments often seek revenues from economic activity, typically through fees or taxes, such as property assessments, customs duties, stamp taxes, value-added assessments, or estate and income taxation. Although the blockchain has libertarian appeal, all competent governments assert the power of taxation broadly. For blockchain or other innovative financial products to evade tax, they would have to do so in ways analogous to how all illegal activities avoid taxation. Because finance is so information-intensive, it is difficult for the tax evader to cover all their digital tracks.

Protecting Existing Interests. Governments often use their power to protect the economic status quo. This is not always bad; supporting principal providers of goods and services can benefit both the enterprises and their consumers. In some cases, incumbent providers may be entrenched by the economics of the situation. For example, Bitcoin miners may be natural monopolies, due to the large fixed costs of capitalizing the power plant for a mining operation. Similarly, a particular digital currency (e.g., Bitcoin versus Bitgold) might become a natural monopoly through network externalities. A common public policy response to limit monopoly-power rent-seeking is to institutionalize the monopoly as a public utility with democratic governance, such as a local water and sewer commission. Not coincidentally, the Bitcoin mine starts to look like a central bank; indeed, central banks, which have extensive experience as governance mechanisms for monetary stability, have taken an active interest in digital currencies[14,15].

At the same time, solidification of the status quo can suppress innovation, by entrenching both incumbent providers and existing processes. Such suppression can be a byproduct of otherwise well-intentioned regulation. Regulators and their charges co-evolve over time, so that the incumbent institutions on one side are typically well adapted to the incumbents on the other. Bank examiners know what to expect from well-run banks, and vice versa. Some argue that public utility treatment can stifle the emergence of competition that would ameliorate a monopoly situation.

Enshrining one set of interests or market participants over another can work both in a positive and negative way. For example, if ex-ante rules designed to ensure proper governance, infrastructure, resilience and so forth have the effect of designating *(de jure or de facto)* a limited, trusted set of miners, confidence in the system and its resilience and potential resolution may increase. But this same motivation could create a set of unintended consequences such as giving the keys to the system to one set of market participants over another. The result could be to undermine confidence in the system by the very rules designed to bolster that confidence. In any case, policymakers will want to watch how the system evolves with an eye toward facilitating the development of a stable system.

Considerations related to enshrining the interests of one over another may be necessary for adoption of blockchain technologies in the financial system, particularly where legal structures have been designed with financial intermediaries in existence or in mind. For example, derivatives markets are presently subject to a new and comprehensive regime to steer transactions to organized exchanges and central clearing at registered clearinghouses. If a blockchain technology develops in these markets allowing for bilateral exchange without the need for centralized trading, clearing, and settlement, changes in law, regulation, and regulatory practice could be required. To avoid regulatory arbitrage, supervisors will need to coordinate in much the same way they have regarding capital requirements for banks, or conduct rules for other market participants. Authorities will need to consider how these activities could be governed so that oversight can continue for the protection of the system.

Mitigating Wider and Secondary Effects. Regulation should consider both immediate goals, and the potential larger effects of an activity. Legal intervention can promote or hinder specific actions, but it can also seek to create systemic effects ranging from efficiency to distributional fairness.

Good rules typically have the goal of helping the users and providers internalize the costs and benefits of an activity. Good rules also try to avoid unnecessary burden, such as onerous reporting requirements. At the federal level, this principle has been codified in a series of executive orders and OMB Circular A-4 (Office of Management and Budget 2003), summarized as directing:

> "Important goals of regulatory analysis are (1) to establish whether federal regulation is necessary and justified to achieve a social goal and (2) to clarify how to design regulations in the most efficient, least burdensome, and most cost-effective manner[16]."

These principles argue for regulatory restraint. Bitcoin's conceit of mimicking a traditional gold standard to put its monetary policy on autopilot has been adequate, but will likely remain adequate only if it does not aspire to go beyond its limited role as a convenient payments medium.

Rules must also be *socially acceptable;* they must "fit" with cultural norms and conditions. In the United States, traditions of personal autonomy and contractual freedom may make some kinds of otherwise plausible regulatory intervention unacceptable. Indeed, the American income tax system is, in many instances, based on self-reporting, not direct government monitoring of transactions and activities that reflect taxable gains. Thus, even if a blockchain technology could embed the ability to capture income tax revenues through payment systems, it's not clear that society would accept such an intrusion. Likewise, an otherwise efficiency-enhancing rule may be unacceptable because it violates conceptions of "fairness." A related concept is *cognitive acceptability.* The counter-intuitive nature of many economic arguments, such as free trade, monetary expansion, and public expenditure in recessions make them hard sells to a public not made up of experts. Blockchain technologies, with a complicated mathematical and technological basis, may suffer similar challenges of understanding.

Another important dimension of innovation is *generativity*, meaning the self-referential modularity that allows some systems to support additional outcomes not envisioned when the system was created. A simple example of this property is LEGO™ blocks, which allow the creation through creative assembly of a nearly limitless set of shapes. A purpose-built scale-model airplane may be more realistic than the LEGO™ version, but it cannot be readily converted to anything else. In the domain of rules, the generative nature of the open architecture of the internet is part of its success[17]; no one foresaw Facebook or Uber at the start.

Blockchain technology, developed initially for Bitcoin, may also be a generative system, insofar as it enables transformation of existing financial systems. Generativity is also a desirable property for the regulation of innovative technologies. That said, there are risks in a generative system. Unanticipated consequences are not always benign, and an open system can be more open to predatory capture. The precautionary principle, which limits the new if there is significant uncertainty around possible harm, would discourage generativity, with its possibility of unintended consequences[18].

Systemic Concerns. What are the government's concerns for financial regulation? In addition to the general goals to prevent harm and to provide frameworks for growth, there are also concerns for systemic stability. Although one or more government bodies (sometimes federal, sometimes state, sometimes both) generally exist to supervise or regulate each of these areas, no one body supervises the entire system. However, the new creations from the financial crisis – the OFR and the Financial Stability Oversight Council (FSOC) – do have this system-wide view.

In some cases, the migration to blockchain would disrupt little in the financial system and its regulatory framework as currently organized. For example, blockchain as a settlement solution could simply replace current digital ledgers while still residing within a narrow distributed ledger controlled by a central repository, similar to a pilot project being explored by Nasdaq[19].

On the other hand, blockchain might deeply disrupt other parts of the system, disintermediating existing participants (perhaps including key players), raising questions about how crucial monitoring, risk management, and resolution activities might transpire in the context of stress episodes.

4. MEANS OF REGULATING: THE "TOOLKIT" FOR REGULATION

Traditional systems of regulation and governance often use a relatively well explored "toolkit" of intervention and constraint. These can be broadly grouped as those that apply in advance of the activity (ex-ante constraints) and those that are applied after the fact (ex post). As an innovation like blockchain technology, or other financial technologies like artificial intelligence, become the basis for a significant portion of our financial transactions, a similarly comprehensive approach can be expected to emerge to govern its players and individual contracts.

The most extreme ex-ante intervention is proscription: an outright ban on a particular activity, which can be linked to a civil or criminal penalty to give it teeth. This ban can be a general one, or a targeted injunction applied in a particular set of circumstances. Less stringent ex-ante approaches include regulation, qualification and oversight, often linked to required "best practices." These ex-ante governance approaches can especially discourage generative innovation, because they typically set an intentionally constrained framework of possible actions and techniques, with little room for maneuver or discovery[20]. This may be appropriate in high-risk or high-consequence circumstances. Ex-ante constraints on behavior also tend strongly to protect incumbents, whose processes are typically well adapted to the rules – indeed, incumbents and the rule sets governing them will often co-evolve to a comfortable equilibrium. Proponents often argue that blockchain approaches in finance will disrupt a suboptimal equilibrium of this sort.

A softer and more flexible form of ex ante regulation involves assuring that minimal quality or conduct standards are satisfied either by the individual actor (for example TSA pre-screening) or system (a self-regulatory organization with approved conduct rules). Registration and licensing can have a beneficial chilling effect on misbehavior, because the possibility of delicensing would threaten participation in a profitable game. Registration systems can be designed to retain flexibility of practice, but are often linked with established approaches. Membership can require one to respect the norms of the club. On the other hand, such systems can act to certify the registrants' reputability to otherwise skeptical users – an example of regulation helping promote an activity. For example, the National Futures Association, a delegated self-regulatory organization, maintains a registration system to certify firms and individuals for participation. In this case, the industry itself has adopted an ex-ante registration mechanism.

Ex post approaches can be more supportive of innovation, because they allow activities to proceed, only imposing penalties if the *outcome* is bad. Ex post penalties can be located in the criminal law, but linked to outcomes and not the activity itself. Anonymous digital payments are not illegal; anonymous digital payments to support a money laundering syndicate may well be. Similarly, non-criminal consequences can be levied. Whether publicly or privately instigated, these civil penalties can include damages and/or suspension of the activity, whether through the removal of a license, an injunction, or some other proceeding.

Regulatory regimes often mix and match these ingredients. The SEC requires registration of issuers, exchanges, and broker dealers. There is licensing, and the possibility of delicensing. There are general prohibitions against fraud, with ex post public and private civil remedies and possible criminal penalties. There are specific requirements for disclosure and reporting, and specific practices approved under safe-harbor rules.

5. INTERNAL REGULATION THROUGH THE TECHNOLOGY ITSELF: CODE AS LAW

When regulating an activity that is essentially technological, such as a blockchain, there is the intriguing possibility of building at least some of the desirable practices of that activity into the technology itself. As Lawrence Lessig famously argued with reference to the internet, the architecture of a technological system makes rules about what it can and cannot do[21]. In a very real sense, code is law for such purposes.

One reason that a blockchain application like Bitcoin has been able to operate with limited legal intervention is that its technical architecture makes it resistant to a wide range of attacks. Nonetheless there is room for an outside authority to confirm that the architecture does what it purports to do, or to add a layer of societal punishment on those who would try to abuse the service, and perhaps to overlay stability of the system by insisting on mechanisms that produce resilience and confidence. The recent hacking of the Ethereum system, discussed more fully below, illuminates these concerns.

This property of internal regulation creates both a challenge and an opportunity for regulators: can they participate in the creation of the system to embed good law into the source code itself? Will the designers welcome the regulators in? Under what circumstances would the regulators thus expose themselves to liability for any bugs that arise? Would this sort of complicity defeat their effectiveness as enforcers of the rules? There is precedent for such cooperation, but there is also precedent for a more antagonistic relationship that could make such involvement difficult.

There can also be systemic effects of a particular architecture that warrant society's intervention. Individuals acting optimally in their parochial self-interest can cumulatively create misbehaviors that emerge only at the system level, such as bank runs, pricing bubbles, or concentrated risk exposures. There is no reason to think that functions located on a blockchain will be naturally immune to such emergent systemic pathologies, as the Bitcoin's Mt. Gox demonstrated in 2013 when the company, at the time controlling 70% of Bitcoin trading[22], proceeded to have over $400 million worth of Bitcoin appropriated and likely stolen. Despite the distributed nature of the Bitcoin blockchain, market conditions caused an unhealthy centralization of resources, and bad actors can exploit such weaknesses. Steps can be taken to minimize the opportunity for such damage by setting up controls around these systemic effects, whether in the technology or alongside it, and is a likely feature in the landscape of future blockchain technologies.

6. WHO REGULATES: FEDERALISM, LAW MAKING, AND REGULATORY AGENCIES

It is worth reviewing where rules originate and how they get enforced. Statutes, enacted by the legislature, are the starting point for most governmentally established regulatory regimes. The United States has a common law legal system, which means that the legislature's law-making power is shared by courts who interpret the law in the course of adjudicating specific disputes. This power is useful in adapting existing legal principles to new circumstances. Thus, even if a statute does not specifically mention a blockchain, courts could nonetheless construe existing legal rules to apply to blockchain-based activity. The backbone of law then provides for more flexible and specific rules, either those created by governments or by private actors themselves. For instance, the early stock exchanges formed before the regulatory agencies that currently oversee them even existed.

Many regulatory regimes, including most of those related to finance, are assigned for oversight to a regulatory body, such as the SEC or the Federal Reserve. These bodies typically receive delegated power to elaborate specific rules to implement the more general mandates defined in the statutes. This rule-making process is another means by which existing governance regimes may be adapted to blockchain applications. Regulators are also frequently the implementation agents for registrations, licensing, inspections, certifications, and other oversight activity, both ex-ante and ex post. When civil or criminal laws have been broken, the Justice Department may also help with enforcement.

In the United States the jurisdictions of States and Territories also have law-making power. Much of the underlying contract and commercial law relevant to the blockchain will be state law. For example, important initiatives at this level include the blockchain enabling law recently adopted in Vermont, and Delaware has launched a blockchain initiative that aims to develop do develop a similarly innovation-friendly legal environment[23]. Where law gets made and enforced is an important element for its possible effects on applications of technology such as blockchain.

III. LAWS OF GENERAL APPLICABILITY; CONTRACTS AND INSTRUMENTS

Against this background, we can now examine how law and regulation may apply to future developments in our financial system. Particular financial innovations, whether based on blockchain, mobile devices, or other technology, will have domain-specific areas of interaction with regulation. They will also often interact with widely shared principles of legal specification.

In this section, we will look first at some of the wider principles with the potential for broad application, with particular attention to those impacting instruments and contracts. In later sections we will look at the more specific use cases of trading markets, identity and systemic monitoring. While there are a number of important areas within financial services to which blockchain technology and other innovations are applicable, we hope that by delving into these selected targets, the reader will be able to extrapolate broader principles of the interaction between regulation and financial technology (particularly in the context of our "whys and hows" of regulation above). As we begin this review, allow us to repeat our caution – reading the future is inherently speculative. Some of what we suggest will come to pass; other aspects will not. We offer this analysis as a starting point for analysis and not as a confident roadmap.

1. ENABLING LEGISLATION I: EXISTING PROVISIONS

Many financial transactions are constructed around contracts and instruments. These are both creatures of legal recognition, and there are well-developed bodies of law in place to deal with paper-based examples. In the United States, much of the basic framework on these questions comes from state law. Contract, property, corporations, negotiable instruments, these all depend on laws of states such as

New York, California, Massachusetts or Delaware for their creation as enforceable rules. In financial markets, there is also a critical overlay of Federal rulemaking, such as the U.S. securities, currency and banking laws and regulations. The trust-creating nature of blockchain technology can substitute for some of what law has traditionally done in this regard, but in our estimation, law and regulation will play an important role in blockchain applications in this area. This section will look first at examples of legal intervention that will enable blockchain activity by codifying its legal effect. Legal regulation will also aim to accomplish the traditional and linked goals of harm prevention and trust building, and this section will examine these as well. In both cases, it will look at existing law and its possible application along with changes that can be anticipated to deal with concerns specific to a blockchain and its operations.

A starting question is the degree to which these existing rules may apply to versions created, stored or even executed via blockchain-enabled digital interaction. A critical existing law is UETA: the Uniform Electronic Transactions Act promulgated by the Uniform Law Commission[24]. This 1999 draft law has been adopted, sometimes with some local variation, in most of the States; notable holdouts include New York and Illinois. UETA provides recognition for transactions recorded and "signed" in digital form, moving beyond paper to authorize digital originals. UETA's Prefatory Note explains its goals and purpose:

> "It is important to understand that the purpose of the UETA is to remove barriers to electronic commerce by validating and effectuating electronic records and signatures. It is NOT a general contracting statute – the substantive rules of contracts remain unaffected by UETA. Nor is it a digital signature statute. To the extent that a State has a Digital Signature Law, the UETA is designed to support and compliment that statute."

While not explicitly aimed at blockchain and the other innovative technologies considered here, UETA's scope would cover much of the world of contracts and instruments to be recorded or executed through a blockchain system. It would not necessarily apply to the recording of one-party declarations that do not have all the characteristics of a transaction.

In the world of corporations and other business enterprises, some states specifically authorize that the bylaws and shares of a corporation, or the operating agreement of a limited liability company, can be expressed in digital originals. For instance, $2.06 (b) of the Vermont Business Corporations Act provides that the bylaws "may be stored or depicted in any tangible or electronic medium"[25]. Vermont has also recently enacted a statute to give explicit evidentiary recognition to blockchain recording.

2. ENABLING LEGISLATION II: PROVISIONS THAT COULD BE ADDED

Enabling provisions like those set out above may usefully apply to contracts and instruments used in a technologically based platform such as a blockchain, but they have mostly been created outside the context of such innovation. To fully unleash the potential of a technology like blockchain for economic commerce and finance, it will probably prove useful to create some targeted law. For instance, the Uniform Commercial Code (UCC) is another widely adopted, state-law approach to recognizing and structuring a variety of commercial practices, including negotiable instruments. "Negotiability" is the property of an instrument intended to be passed from one owner to the next by a process of assignment that classically involved making the obligation be owed initially to "the order" of a particular person or company. That person, in turn, can make the check, note, or other instrument payable or due to a new holder by endorsement (traditionally through signature) and a direction that it is now, in turn, payable, etc. to the order of that new holder. The magic words "to the order of" create this progressive negotiability, until an eventual holder cashes the check, demands payment under the note, or otherwise calls in the underlying bargain contained in the instrument.

Much of this process could be run through a blockchain mechanism of successive ownership. For instance, ownership transfer of a virtual or actual currency on a blockchain could do much of what a check accomplishes without needing a bank in the middle. Here the blockchain substitutes a somewhat different process for classic negotiation. To get better legal recognition, the practice would benefit from a specific set of rules in the UCC, either as an amendment to the existing provisions on negotiation or, perhaps more fruitfully, as a new Article under the UCC itself.

Escrow arrangements through blockchain could also benefit from specific recognition. If you layer a digital triggering mechanism of some kind onto a blockchain currency transfer, you have created something that looks a lot like a traditional escrow agreement. As with negotiation, however, full implementation cries out for a set of rules for such arrangements that are tailored to the blockchain, and not just borrowed from other contexts with resulting gaps and compromises.

As these examples demonstrate, capturing the potential of blockchain as a vehicle for expressing and executing contracts and instruments will benefit from drafting and enacting well thought out enabling provisions. Rather than standing away from traditional law, blockchain proponents should seek to collaborate with law drafting bodies to develop intelligent solutions that could be enacted on a broad basis in the United States and beyond.

3. HARM PREVENTION AND TRUST BUILDING I: APPLICATIONS OF CURRENT LAW

As we have repeatedly stressed in this chapter, the tasks of building trust in an application and of preventing harm in its use, whether through predation or carelessness, often go hand in hand. The workings of financial markets can be opaque, even to relative experts, and blockchain technology even more so. Both can be seen as "credence goods," where many users have to believe in the honesty of providers without having the ability to monitor them competently[26,27]. Markets in credence goods are often enhanced by the intervention of a respected regulatory structure, rather than impeded by regulatory drag. Much of the regulation of the issuance and trading of financial contracts and instruments is aimed in this domain of harm prevention and trust enhancement, and large portions of this existing regulatory regime can be expected to apply to uses of blockchain for these purposes.

Fraud – active predation through the use of misleading facts or the suppression of relevant information – is a classic target for preventative regulation in financial markets. The anti-fraud provisions of the U.S. securities laws are numerous and have wide application. Some are classic ex-post punishments for fraudulent activity in the sale or purchase of a security. Securities, in this context, cover a wide range of financial contracts and instruments, and would include versions that use blockchain technology just as much as those that are paper based. The most prominent of these ex-post punishment provisions comes under Section 10b of the 1934 Exchange Act and its implementation in Rule 10b-5, which provides:

"It shall be unlawful for any person, directly or indirectly, by the use of any means or instrumentality of interstate commerce, or of the mails or of any facility of any national securities exchange,

> (a) To employ any device, scheme, or artifice to defraud,
>
> (b) To make any untrue statement of a material fact or to omit to state a material fact necessary in order to make the statements made, in the light of the circumstances under which they were made, not misleading, or
>
> (c) To engage in any act, practice, or course of business which operates or would operate as a fraud or deceit upon any person,

in connection with the purchase or sale of any security."

To the extent any of the persons involved in a blockchain-based securities transaction are located in the United States, the blockchain itself would probably count as an "instrumentality of interstate commerce," as would any other technology-based market or transaction platform. This rule creates liability for civil and criminal penalties by the government as well as a civil cause of action for the individuals and businesses harmed by the conduct. There is little doubt that a fraudulent blockchain transaction for securities that met the definitions and jurisdictional requirements of 10b-5 could and would be prosecuted under current law.

And 10b-5 is hardly the only law that could be invoked in case of blockchain fraud. There is a general federal law against "wire fraud" (18 U.S. Code §1343) that would probably apply (the internet or other vehicle for the chain providing the wire), and a number of state anti-fraud provisions.

In addition to the ex-post penalties, there are a number of reporting and information requirements under the securities laws that would apply just as much to blockchain-based activity as to paper-based. Filing and disclosure requirements are pervasive in a securities law context. For instance, if there is the issuance of securities in a company via the blockchain, this could trigger the need for a registration under the Securities Act of 1933 in the same way that a traditional offering would. In a more specific context, when a person acquires more than 5% of a class of publicly traded securities in a public company, this triggers the need to file a Schedule 13D that discloses information about the acquirer. Again, this would apply to acquisitions of blockchain-based interests, without regard to the anonymity that could otherwise be built into the operation of the platform. In a further example, ownership, purchases and sales of securities by corporate insiders, defined as a company's officers and directors, and beneficial owners of more than ten percent of the company's registered equity securities can trigger reports on SEC Forms 3, 4 or 5. Whatever the hope for anonymity, such reports would be trigged by blockchain-based trades that met the other criteria.

A further tactic taken under existing securities law approaches involves requiring and certifying structures of private governance. This approach to "self-regulatory organizations" was set up under the Securities Exchange Act of 1934 and originally applied to securities markets like the New York Stock Exchange and to the National Association of Securities Dealers. More recent mergers and reorganizations have led to other organizations like the Financial Industry Regulatory Authority. The idea is to let the organizations propose and report on their operations and governance rules and regulations, subject to the approval of the SEC. The premise is that the organizations will know the needs of their business better than a regulator would, and should be the source of the governance approach; indeed because many of these self-regulatory organizations are now commercial actors which compete with one another – for example the market exchanges or central clearing houses – they are incentivized to offer competitive products that are also viewed as safe and fair to the market actors that could choose to do business in a competitor's market. The regulator, on the other hand, can keep an eye out for abusive or otherwise objectionable practices that might find their way into the operations notwithstanding the alignment of interests. Flexibility and generativity are provided for, while still avoiding predation and building trust.

One could imagine the extension of this approach to blockchain providers, with a financial utility like the Bitcoin blockchain setting up its own structures of process and operation, but still requiring regulatory oversight and review.

4. HARM PREVENTION AND TRUST BUILDING II: DEVELOPING NEW LAW

Existing laws and regulations cannot do the entire job here either. New rules for preventing harm and building trust will be needed to deal with blockchain specific challenges. For instance, the ability to set up automatically executing contracts that cannot be rescinded is sometimes offered as an advantage blockchain technology could provide. That said, there may be circumstances of fraud or mistakes where undoing the non-rescindable may be a necessity. How do you build a "reset button" into a blockchain platform and keep the integrity that is a core part of it? Would it involve airgaps and "ask the human to execute it" moments? What is the legal review and intervention that might be needed to trigger such a circumstance? Contracts frequently contain "severability" clauses which allow the contract to survive even where a particular offending clause is struck by virtue of a court decision. In such a case, could the code be written to allow to the contract to function even without that clause or, if not, could the contract be opened to have the rest rewritten so that it operates as newly intended? These questions are explored more fully in Section IV below.

As new products are developed, new rules may be needed. We are still often envisioning financial innovations such as blockchain technology as better ways of doing things we already know about; we are only just beginning to anticipate the really new things that they could do in setting up and executing agreements and legally active instruments. Disruptive change is happening, but is hard to predict in advance. What we can anticipate is that law will be called on to do many of the things it already does to make a new technology trustworthy.

5. COORDINATION AND STANDARD SETTING

A final area for government activity at a general level is providing mechanisms for coordination and standard setting on the software that can be used to power the platforms and to express the terms of contracts and instruments in executable code. While simply mandating such standards could be attempted, by and large the government seeks to be a catalyst and convener to help private actors come to agreement around common standards. The National Institute for Science and Technology plays such a role, and this kind of activity with respect to the financial markets is part of the mandate of the Office of Financial Research.

A possible set of steps in this direction would be the development of a "Legal Specification Language" with the capacity to express and execute the permutations of event and consequence which are central to many contracts and instruments. Such a language would move blockchain technology from being a relatively passive ledger for establishing records of transactions to a platform on which their design and execution are carried out. "Smart contracts" and "smart securities" would become quickly computable objects in an ecosystem of like specifications. Elements of this language and system exist; creating the complete package will take not only time and effort but also the kind of coordination and standard development processes in which government can take an active and useful role.

6. TECHNO-LEGAL ASPECTS OF SMART CONTRACTS

Smart contracts have received interest among the internet technical community due to a number of promising capabilities, as an extension of the basic blockchain system found in the Bitcoin system. A smart contract today is seen as an *executable code* that is designed to run on specific computing architectures. A given smart contract may be designed to execute on one computer (i.e. one node in the blockchain system), or it may be designed to run concurrently with other related copies of itself, or other smart contracts that are related to (or derived from) itself. The execution of a group of smart contracts may be designed to occur simultaneously at one time, or they may be designed to occur in a cascading or interleaved fashion. These modes of execution may have dramatic significant to the outcome of the contract as a unit.

Another dimension of the smart contract paradigm is the fact that multiple parties are involved in the actual execution of the contract. These entities include: the originator of the smart contract; the computer/node owner or operator where the contract runs; external data sources; and the counterparty in the contract. These entities may or may not reside within the same legal jurisdiction.

Today there are a number of open technical issues with regards to smart contracts that may carry legal implications, such as authenticated data sources, correct and complete execution, forensics and post-event evidence, and cross-jurisdiction smart contract executions. All of these are possible targets for the kind of standard-setting activity in which government can play an important role. A detailed discussion of these elements is beyond the scope of this book, but may be addressed by the authors in a future document.

IV. SPECIFIC USE CASE I: TRANSACTION RECORDS AND TRADING MARKETS

Several efforts have been made to use new technologies to change how securities are issued and traded, such as WIT Capital or WR Hambrecht, but have failed to deliver a compelling enough value proposition to current market participants to induce widespread change. With the rise of blockchain-based technologies, even the leaders of the world's largest incumbent stock exchanges are now acknowledging a threat to status quo. This section will examine a few critical issues relating to technological innovation in the issuance and trading of securities, and will explore possible regulatory responses to these challenges.

1. ISSUANCE AND TRADING IN A BLOCKCHAIN CONTEXT

Most stocks and bonds are issued as securities with known and recorded ownership. This is certainly the case since the 1982 TEFRA prohibited the issuance of U.S. bearer bonds[27]. Security ownership recordation is, at core, a process of recording a "fact" with distributed, shared agreement on its truth. Because a blockchain manages consensus version of the truth, an appropriately designed blockchain could, in principle, be well suited to the tasks of securities transfer and ownership recording, and have the potential to make the process more accurate and efficient. In addition, the distributed nature of blockchain may create a greater sense of trust in the system, as any participant in the market can validate a transaction, and regulatory oversight becomes easier because of an irrevocable ledger that is readily accessed. After issuance, much of the life of a security exists in secondary markets. Thus, demonstration of exclusive ownership and transfer becomes paramount, just as in a currency implementation of blockchain. The linked issue of *identity*, which must also be solved for a recordation system to make sense, will be addressed later in this chapter.

Permissioned blockchains can solve for issues of identity of participants and exclusivity of ownership. The Bitcoin blockchain (BCBC) protocol is less suited to this purpose, as it strives to maintain the anonymity of participants, in an effort to mimic old-fashioned cash (specie or paper currency) payments. A *propos* of the TEFRA note above, ownership identification is required for numerous purposes, including property taxes and taxes on capital gains, so a permissioned or identified system will be needed. However, systems have already been proposed (by MIT among others) for privacy-protected, traceable transactions – identity could be managed by a trusted third party but the identity of a particular participant in a transaction could be cryptographically shielded. This system would allow for anonymous trading of beneficial ownership unless and until an appropriately permissioned event (e.g. a warrant is issued by a duly recognized court of authority), at which point the guardian entity managing identity could selectively release the required information.

How do we decide who is "inside the wall" – i.e., who gets to write blocks to the blockchain? Given that advance knowledge of the index is valuable (tradable) information, who gets to read the blocks on the chain as the consensus is being formed? Some versions of permissioned blockchains allow a small set of trusted participants to trade with each other – akin to a private trading network. Yet, this would have an exclusionary effect on small investors. It is also possible to create a permissioned, public blockchain where only some have "write access", but anyone can "read" the transaction stream, and this may provide for the balance required between competing objectives.

What do we do in the case of errors of execution? The BCBC, and most other blockchains, do not have a convenient "undo" mechanism when mistakes are made. For example, a minor programming error forced Knight Capital to sell itself after losing $440 million at a rate of $10 million a minute[28]. To avoid this, one might impose stringent authentication on participants, but this too would deviate from the original BCBC protocol of user anonymity. In the case of error, it is possible to inject a "correcting entry", but the counterparties would need to agree to this – if Snidely decided he liked his erroneous transfer, it would be difficult to undo absent a court order (and even then, that simply creates a legal claim).

This concern is illuminated by a dramatic blockchain failure that occurred in June, 2016. This time, Ethereum was the context for an attack by a hacker, using the nom de fraude "the Attacker[29]." This would-be bandit exploited a programming flaw in a digital currency fund called the DAO (decentralized autonomous organization) to direct the transfer of 3.6 million ETH (then worth about $53 million) into his account. The co-founder of Ethereum countered by freezing the DOA tokens. The Attacker then added insult to injury by asserting, through a post on Pastebin, that he/she had a valid claim to the money, arguing that the record in the Ethereum chain was the only source for title, and that any attempt to change the record would be a breach of the rules. Even though the Attacker threatened to unleash lawyers on those seeking to correct the fraud, reverse hackers allied to the platform managed to recapture most of the funds[30].

The resort to cyber vigilantes to battle back from predatory exploitation of the system's architecture suggests that trusting the technology as a substitute for authoritative governance can be a losing strategy. Rather, creating some kind of reconciliation or correction capability looks increasingly to be a necessary element of a blockchain-based trading system. Such a capacity ultimately needs an adjudicator; in a traditional market or contract we look to choice of law and choice of forum provisions to set up the correction system. We can also specify *private* adjudication, through arbitration or some kind of market specific committee. The choices are several; the need to have one in place is critical.

2. SETTLEMENT AND HYPOTHECATION

The settlement of a trade is an area currently burdened with several layers of process, much of which predates the advent of electronic records, and thus has the potential to be automated using blockchain technology. Much of securities settlement involves statements of ownership – of stocks, bonds, etc. This is broadly consistent with the original BCBC, which tracks uninterrupted ownership of specific coins through time. In part, this works because the individual coins are clearly defined and identified, and ownership is rivalrous. It makes sense that, at every instant, there is a one-to-one mapping between a coin and its owner, and that one should be able to track an individual coin's ownership relationships uninterrupted through time. Moreover, to the extent that a registrar's blockchain uses a distributed ledger, the BCBC has a mining cost that can be calibrated to encourage truthful voting under a distributed consensus protocol. A number of blockchain variations would be capable of managing such a distributed ledger of ownership.

For some legal applications, a document's chain of custody is important. An analog to this is the chain of obligation for reused or rehypothecated collateral. Unmanaged rehypothecation chains – the Lehman collateral hairball – were an important factor in the September 2008 run. Collateral rehypothecation frequently occurs in bilateral OTC markets. A trusted, decentralized registration point for OTC collateral pledges could therefore be an especially valuable application for an appropriately managed blockchain. However, the ability for accurate identification and authentication (which can be made to be present in permissioned blockchains but absent from the BCBC blockchain) would be crucial to make this work reliably.

Scalability is also a critical issue. The BCBC protocol manages a distributed transaction ledger, so that the current state of an individual's "account" must be calculated by rolling forward all historical transactions. Because current inventories of cash and securities are key variables in the settlement process, this calculation would need to be performed often. It is not clear that this process will scale adequately, especially in markets, such as equities, where high-frequency trading is dominant. Some solutions to blockchain scalability have suggested creating "sub consensus" nodes that aggregate to a larger consensus – but this only exacerbates the coordination issue cited earlier.

Similarly, the BCBC protocol does not directly support fungibility of cash and securities, relying instead on a relatively clumsy process of excessive lump-sum transfer, followed by a mining and return of "change" in the appropriate amount. This introduces a coordination burden to ensure that these two messages are recognized as countermanding components of the same legal transaction. In principle, this should be straightforward and feasible, but *practical experience*[31] shows that financial markets are not always capable of keeping related transactions aligned. Disputes should be expected in practice, and some dispute-resolution mechanism will be needed. It would be hypothetically possible to train a machine-mediated dispute resolution system to facilitate efficiency, but it might not be feasible (at least in the near term) to eliminate human intervention entirely.

We have seen occasional flash-crashes in a range of markets using high-frequency algorithmic trading. In many cases, the trading venue has intervened to clamp trading and cancel executed transactions. This involves the unilateral reversal by a third party (the exchange) of "completed" legal agreements. Clearly, this is not an optimal state of affairs, but conditional on a flash crash, unilateral intervention to cancel contracts is preferable to most alternatives. However, this requires a trusted relationship outside of the relationship between the transacting parties themselves, and some form of effective delegated authority permitting the trading venue to act pursuant to a set of pre-determined rules, or with the ex post involvement of authorities. Blockchain technologies also have the "undo" issues cited previously – it was designed as an irrevocable ledger, so unwinding errors becomes cumbersome to say the least.

3. TRANSACTION MONITORING

A blockchain defines a consensus version of the truth. In practice, we should expect to see an ecosystem of many blockchains, large and small, defining various "local truths" for specific communities and purposes. The movement to give blockchains legal standing as evidence in contract enforcement is progressing, with the Vermont statute discussed in the textbox standing as an early beacon. In such a world, it is inevitable that two competing blockchain systems will eventually announce conflicting versions of the "truth." It is possible that the blockchain consensus mechanism itself will step in to harmonize the differences. However, this will not always happen, because the consensus preference in each community may be to tolerate the inconsistency. Once again, this creates a need for a reconciliation mechanism. Industry coordination efforts such as Hyperledger and Interledger need to take into account the nuances of financial securities' specific implications, and/or a new coordinating action will need to be taken around securities transactions to allow for reconciliation.

Suppose that industry blockchains successfully perform much of the low-level data validation work that is currently handled by traditional double-entry bookkeeping and back-office confirmation and reconciliation processes. These blockchains could then be central staging points for supervision by regulatory bodies, archival recording, and enforcement of market manipulation laws. This raises issues including: how much access systemic supervisors have to these details without intruding on individual privacy, under what circumstances should supervisors be allowed to escalate their access, and who gets to decide whether escalation is permitted.

V. SPECIFIC USE CASE II: IDENTITY, TRUST AND DATA SECURITY IN A BLOCKCHAIN ENVIRONMENT

As noted elsewhere in this chapter, the financial services industry must be able to provide its core services to the rest of the economy, and the stability of the system – to be able to provide these services – relies upon trust in the system, resilience and reliability, and robustness to manipulation. Blockchain technology promises much, but it may need to be coupled with existing and emerging technologies that improve identity management and information security for it to meet systemic requirements.

1. CURRENT INFRASTRUCTURE

Our financial system relies upon an often disparate network of networks and systems for its infrastructure built up over time. These networks must identify instruments and parties in precise and unambiguous ways to move money or settle securities. One such network is the payment system managed by the Society for Worldwide Interbank Financial Transfers (SWIFT) which moves massive sums of money between central banks and major financial institutions. Like so many infrastructures underpinning our financial system – whether they are designed to facilitate trade or investment, payment systems, risk transfer platforms, or others – the SWIFT system relies upon an unambiguous and robust-to-fraud ability to precisely identify counterparties and transactors.

SWIFT relies upon an identification code – the BIC or Business Identifier Code – to gain this precision. But the financial system more broadly lacks an unambiguous and ubiquitous means of identity management. For decades disparate identification systems built up in our financial markets. Vendors provided proprietary partial solutions, such as in the CUSIP (which identifies individual securities), the Dunn and Bradstreet

DUNS number, or the Markit Red Code (to identify reference entities in Credit Default Swaps). Each different and covering a portion of the world's financial market participants, these vended solutions have proven costly and of limited use outside of internal systems because of intellectual property limitations.

Unlike the emergence of a superior product that effectively sets the market standard, no superior product emerged for entity identification, and financial interests encouraged these proprietary standards to remain proprietary, allowing the standard owner to fully benefit from the economic rent. And although all users of data made openly available and conforming to a common standard would benefit from reform, individual players examining their costs and the benefits of a cooperative system could not justify the costs of creating a global system. Moreover, because a global system would be a natural monopoly with large network externalities, these private players would be unlikely to cooperate without some external compulsion. A recent effort of authorities from around the globe has sought to solve this problem by creating a "Legal Entity Identifier" which has now been adopted by over 400,000 entities in 195 countries[32]. This development is a good example of a productive use of the convening power of government.

In the case of these identity management systems, whether a closed, proprietary system, such as the BIC, or an open system, such as the LEI, the ability to rely on the identifier is paramount. Market participants and the authorities that oversee them and these markets require the ability to know "who is who" in our markets. Also critical is the need to have these identification systems interoperate, especially as markets become more interconnected. The interoperability will aid oversight and risk management systems by allowing exposures to be aggregated and netted, reduce opportunities for error or fraud, and generally improve the ability to have confidence in markets and other infrastructures. But how does this confidence arise? How do we become confident that we are dealing with the "who" we have understood to be dealing with?

Different approaches could be applied to this problem. One approach is self-identification. This may work well where the incentives to accurately self-identify are high and the costs of remedy are low. Self-identification may also work where a counterparty has the opportunity to conduct whatever diligence is due to manage the risk of mis-identification (or other information about the counterparty like credit risk). This may be a sufficient approach where the costs of remedy (such as expensive litigation) are high. Likewise, in a closed system with repeat transactions, the incentives to self-identify accurately are sufficiently high, the costs imposed upon inaccurate identification are also high, self-identification may also be sufficient.

But self-identification is also often coupled with a trusted source. That source could come from a government – a driver's license or social security card – or an institution (such as the SWIFT system, another market participant with skin in the game like a credit provider, or perhaps a distributed system of verification). This trusted source of entity verification can be a proxy for the expensive due diligence regime described above. In each of these cases the level of assurance necessary (given the risk or costs of remediation) is measured against the level of trust and proof provided.

In a distributed system, where would the source of proof come from and would it be sufficient given the risks and costs of remediation? Different approaches can be envisioned, including limited blockchain networks (much like the SWIFT network), where entry into the system requires some level of proving up as a condition of entry. In such a system, who would be the gatekeeper, and how could such a gatekeeper be trusted?

One source of analogy is the registration system currently existent in our markets, where exchanges and other market infrastructures are required to meet certain quality and fairness conditions set by regulators before gaining registration and their associated prominent role. Oversight, carried out through inspections, examinations, heightened sanctions regimes, and books and records requirements, is used to assure both initial and continued compliance with whatever trust rules have been set to assure confidence in the system.

In other regimes, economic forces and liability regimes provide the trust infrastructure. Such an example can be found in dark pools, where closed networks of large traders operate in an opaque-by-design way that protects anonymity. The host of the pool has sufficient regulatory and legal exposure to give the participants confidence that while they may not know the identity of their counterparties, they can rely upon their bids and offers. Blockchain implementations would not need different mechanisms than these existing ones to manage counterparty identification.

But what of more open systems which are perhaps not centrally managed or regulated but instead operate as many advocates of blockchain technology would envision, e.g., as peer-to-peer? In such a system, participants can certainly self-identify but counterparties will want assurance of identity. The distributed network could use the network to provide proof, perhaps using a hierarchal system of proof-checking standards (for example, the existence of agreed-upon third party proof sources) to assure identity. In such cases, self identification is certainly possible but presents problems of, not just fraud exposure, but even appropriate tactics designed to avoid market shifts by concealing a beneficial owner of shares, "which" could make the jobs of risks managers and regulators very difficult.

At a minimum, if an entity using blockchain technology in a regulated market seeks anonymity, authorities and the courts will require identification capable of revelation at some point. So the technology will need to provide this flexibility of assured legitimacy of counterparty even in an anonymous transaction, coupled with the ability to reveal that identity. Of course, this begs questions about who can unlock this information, under what circumstances, and how those authorities (courts, regulators or self-regulatory institutions) can gain the keys and have certainty that the keys will work.

Interconnections in our financial services system are critical to understand for risk management, to undertake supervisory firms and market monitoring, and to value investments and gauge counterparty risks. These interconnections can explain how risks propagate through our system and they can demonstrate structural points of concentration and potential failure. Understanding how a failure of a market – for example the overnight funding market – could affect a particular firm which is exposed to still other firms is critical for financial stability oversight. These "who owns whom" and "who owns what" questions are revealed by linking the identified entities to their corporate sisters through regulatory filings, or linking them to counterparties through illiquid instruments. Blockchain technologies have been proposed to do just these things, such as through smart contracts that could represent a derivatives agreement for example. And thus, just as common identification standards and governance frameworks are needed for entity identification, instruments and the links between them will need common standards in blockchain systems with governance mechanisms that give assurance to firms and supervisors that the links reveal precise and actionable information.

There are many complexities to these arrangements. For example, ownership may exist by virtue of a clear language in a regulatory filing or corporate ownership agreement, but it could also exist by virtue of a springing interest that operates by virtue of external factors or demands. It could also exist by virtue of economic interests such as a minority shareholder interest that is viewed by regulators as a controlling interest. Technologies such as blockchain that would seek to represent these interests would need to be dynamic and may also need to allow for hidden interests that the distributed network could only see on some decisions by either the holder of the interest or an overseer. Such complexities reveal difficult questions about governance and one can expect that authorities will expect that the system is capable about responding to these complexities.

2. SECURITY WITHIN BLOCKCHAINS: REGULATORY AND MARKET NEEDS

Just as market participants and supervisors need assurance that the information in the financial system is accurate and actionable, so too do they require that the information technologies that undergird it are resilient and secure. American financial markets are considered among the best in the world because of the emphasis on fairness and transparency, but even these markets sometimes suffer from concerns about unequal access and treatment. A system relying on blockchain technology will need to provide certain basic trustworthy security and resilience features, but it could enable improvements over existing infrastructures that suffer from single points of failure and "weakest link" problems.

Such a weak link problem revealed itself in recent news of the penetration of the interbank payment system managed by SWIFT, the consortium owned by banks that moves money between banking institutions and central banks. According to press reports, SWIFT's client software was penetrated and the breach was used to divert money from the Bangladeshi Central Bank's account at the New York Federal Reserve Bank to casinos and elsewhere in the Philippines. The attempted heist was almost $1 billion, and most was thwarted, but almost $1 million remains missing. Some weeks later a second attempted hack was blocked only because a spelling error alerted someone of the potential for fraud. What is notable about these attacks is not just the existence of cyber fraud to steal huge sums of money, but the potential implications for financial stability if this backbone of our financial system loses credibility. Fortunately, the 3,000 institutions that own SWIFT and its 11,000 users are highly motivated to prevent further damage. SWIFT is a closed system, designed to be secure. But the weak point was the Bangladeshi Central Bank's SWIFT software portal, which was compromised by a fraudster gaining entry using stolen credentials.

Robustness to manipulation is certainly a concern, but perhaps more central to the ability of a blockchain infrastructure to function would be its resilience to cyber attack. Blockchain implementations will need design decisions that minimize the ability of a node of the system to disrupt the whole through penetration, the unleashing of malware, denials of service or so forth.

A registration-type regime may well be suited to providing these assurances to participants, but this approach requires adequate understanding on the part of the regulatory community, as well as full access to the critical nodes of the system. Notably, SEC disclosure laws create a requirement that public companies disclose material risks.

Annual reports are now replete with discussions of the impact cyber threats have on businesses, but the information in these disclosures may be weakened by the legitimate need of the company to protect confidence in its ability to defend against these threats. And entities that are not public would not be subject to such disclosures.

And when an attack on a blockchain system does occur, who will step in to fight against the attack and under what authority and access regime? How will this access occur if parts of the distributed network reside outside of regulatory reach? Given that money doesn't flow to marketplaces that are viewed as unsafe or unfair, it could be that participants in such a blockchain market would require that the system be available to supervision and subject to understood rules. This puts more pressure on authorities to understand these blockchain technologies and their proponents to provide clear, verifiable information regarding their security and resilience.

3. IDENTITY WITHIN BLOCKCHAINS: CURRENT LIMITATIONS AND POSSIBLE SOLUTIONS

There is currently tremendous interest in the role of digital identities within blockchain systems, in particular with "public" blockchains (permissionless blockchains) as exemplified by the Bitcoin system and its underlying blockchain. One of the most cited positive features of the Bitcoin system is its use of "self-asserted identities", meaning that any individual or entity can simply create a public key-pair and begin using it to transact in Bitcoin in a pseudonymous way. This interest in self-asserted identities arises from a general social concern about the diminishing control that individuals have today in the privacy of their data in an increasingly connected world.

However, the notion of a self-issued digital identity has an inherent limitation in terms of scalability. This scalability limitation is not only present in the Bitcoin currency system and its blockchain, but it is also present in the PGP system[33] where a user self-issues their PGP key-pair. The user as the key-holder must provide their PGP public-key directly to their friends and colleagues, either in-person or through a public "key ownership declaration" event (e.g. "PGP key signing parties" at IETF face-to-face meetings).

Furthermore, the current self-issued digital identities (in the form of self-generated public-key pairs) does not scale because it lacks integration with existing infrastructures -- both digital infrastructures and real-world infrastructures. A complete and scalable identity management system needs to ground identity in the physical world, and must not rely solely and unconditionally on existing identity/service providers. We believe a new model is needed for "self-sourced identities" that provide privacy-preservation as well as scalability at the global internet level.

A key feature of new scalable models of identity is that they must allow entities in the ecosystem to (i) verify the "quality" of an identity, and (ii) to assess the relative "freedom" or independence of an identity from any given authority (e.g. government, businesses, etc.), and (iii) to assess the source of trust for a digital identity.

If anonymity is a requirement for self-source identities to fulfill the needs of user privacy, then true anonymity in digital identities requires more than self-issuance of a public key-pair (as it is the case today in the Bitcoin blockchain system). It requires that the identity also possess the feature of unlinkability across transactions, preventing personal information leakage through correlation attacks. And even if a digital identity has anonymity and unlinkability, it still requires the relying party (counterparty) to accept the identity. That is, the relying party must be able to assess the provenance and source of trust of a given anonymous self-sourced identity. Consequently future self-sourced identity systems must incorporate the notion of the varying degree of quality of the identity as a function of the varying degrees of the veracity of the provenance information (i.e. source of trust) underlying the identity.

4. DIGITAL IDENTITIES AND ATTRIBUTES FOR FUTURE BLOCKCHAIN SYSTEMS

There are a number of possible avenues that can be pursued for scalable identity management and federation purposes. In seeking to achieve the desirable characteristics of digital identities and attributes, different forms of blockchain technologies and components may need to be invented or introduced. These include new economic models for remunerating entities participating in the ecosystem, as well as new proof-of-work schemes that are efficient in completing tasks.

(a) *Verifiable pseudonymous identities and attributes:* Anonymous and verifiable identities have been a topic of research for over two decades now[34]. Some of these schemes have been implemented in systems such as U-Prove47[35] and IdeMix 45[36], and some limited deployments have been carried out[37]. These proposed systems have not seen broad deployment in the internet due to a number of constrains (e.g. lack of use cases or business models). The arrival of the Bitcoin system and the potential of new forms of blockchain-based systems may provide use cases of the deployment of these existing anonymous and verifiable identities.

(b) *Smart-contracts for binding and revealing attributes:* A node on the blockchain P2P network has the capability to compute smart contracts, which are sequences of computations that map to legal agreements (e.g. between two transacting entities). The same computation model can be developed further to allow attributes (regarding a pseudonymous identity) to be bound to a contract that names the pseudonymous identity. The computation could begin with attributes that are "blinded" and then subsequently release one or more of the attributes during the multi-round smart contract exchange protocol. In this way the multi-round negotiations can build up towards a release of all the relevant attributes regarding both sides of the transaction. Examples of such contracts include bidding at auctions, which could start with an anonymous or pseudonymous buyer/bidder accompanied by attributes of the buyer (e.g. buyer financial worth, history of bidding, etc.).

One innovation that could contribute to reliable identity management in future blockchain systems is data-driven distributed computation to derive attributes: in this approach the P2P distributed nodes on a blockchain would each collect data regarding an identity and perform analytics based on the data available to each node. Each node would first arrive at a "sub-attribute" value or parameter (e.g. single credit score) independently of the other nodes. Collectively the nodes would then contribute their respective sub-attributes into a group computation process (such as a Multi-Party Computation algorithm) that would result in a complete attribute. If a privacy-preserving algorithm is used for the MPC, then there will be the added benefit that no single node will know the sub-attributes from the other nodes. Proposed solutions such as Enigma[38] can provide the foundation for deriving attributes. This of course would need to be reversible for the reasons articulated previously.

Another opportunity lies in the legal aspects of identities and attributes on the blockchain, namely the introduction of a legal trust framework that uses automated contracts exchange (smart contracts or otherwise) to reduce friction in using digital identities through the blockchain. Such frameworks aim at the reduction of risk and liabilities of entities in the ecosystem through a set of agreed principles; operating rules and mechanisms for legal recourse. Legal trust frameworks are crucial to the acceptance of digital identities and attributes in the real-world. Some examples of legal trust frameworks for identity management and federation are FICAM[39], OpenID Exchange[40] and Safe-BioPharma[41].

5. SCALABLE DIGITAL IDENTITIES: ADDRESSABILITY, TRUST SOURCE AND VERIFIABLE ATTRIBUTES

There are a number of desirable characteristics for digital identities that can guide future blockchain innovation around identity management. If satisfied, these characteristics could meet the regulatory needs described above.

> (a) *Addressability:* The notion of addressability refers not only to the uniqueness of an identity string at a global scale, but also the semantics embedded within the identity structure that allows it to be used in a functional way. For example, the current "email identity" consists of a name (unique within the namespace of the domain) followed by a fully qualified domain name. These semantics allow protocols such as SMTP (Simple Mail Transfer Protocol) and POP3 protocols to interpret the identity as a routable email address.

(b) *Source of Trust:* The source of trust of an identity (within a namespace) is derived or bequeathed from the authoritative entity that owns and/or manages that namespace. In essence, the source of trust vouches for the named identity, namely that the identity truly exists and is associated with an individual or entity. For example, the social security number of a U.S. citizen is bequeathed by the government as the authoritative entity governing the SSN namespace. The email address of a person is made available by the email service provider as the legal entity that owns the corresponding domain namespace. A digital certificate legally issued (signed) by a PKI service provider to a user is done under the authority of the PKI provider as specified in the service contract (referred to as the certificate Practices Statement or CPS). The notion of a source of trust is crucial from the perspective of the legal acceptability of the digital identity within online transactions especially when transactions cross boundaries between the digital and real world. The legal aspects of identity management within an ecosystem is typically expressed through a legal trust framework, which is a set of legal processes and operating rules for the issuance, management, accreditation of identities and identity providers within that ecosystem.

(c) *Verifiable Attributes:* Related to the source of trust of an identity is the source of trust or authority regarding attributes associated with the digital identity. The source of trust for an attribute is typically called the attribute authority. The attribute authority "binds" (e.g. cryptographically) an attribute to a digital identity. In many instances, there may be several authoritative sources of an attribute, each making assertions with different degrees of veracity. The Relying Party in a transaction is the entity that ultimately decides whether to accept or reject a given assertion regarding an identity. For example, a state government may be an attribute authority for the residency status of a person (e.g. "Joe is a legal resident of Massachusetts"). A private banking consortium may be the attribute authority for some financial information regarding an identity (e.g. "Joe has a FICO score above 500 pts").

(d) *Privacy Preserving:* A digital identity scheme should preserve the privacy of its owner. Currently, identities in the form of email addresses are designed for addressability at the expense of privacy. Self-issued identities in the Bitcoin systems and PGP system provides a degree of privacy but at the expense of scalability. New paradigms, such as the ability to create an opt-in anonymous identity on a permissioned blockchain, with anonymous verification and the ability of a regulator following due process to reveal identity, help bridge these schemes.

VII. SPECIFIC USE CASE III: BLOCKCHAIN, STABILITY AND SYSTEMIC OVERSIGHT

Our discussions so far have focused on the needs of authorities and market participants in their direct activities, and on rules that can help to facilitate the adoption of blockchain and other financial technologies in a productive and protective way. Equally important is whether the technology and the legal framework can be adapted so that authorities, market participants, and the courts can address or avoid failures during periods of stress to the stability of the system. These solutions include suitable points of entry for policy tools such as liquidity infusions, the presence of interested Samaritans to guarantee, backstop or restart market activities given failures or loss of confidence, and the possibility to unwind transactions and resolve failed institutions, markets or processes.

Our consideration of these challenges falls into two principal categories: (i) the abstraction, evaluation, and analysis of data from a systemic perspective and (ii) mechanisms for crisp and effective action, systemically, particularly in times of stress or crisis. In traditional financial markets and transactions, these two functions have been the domain of a small group of regulatory bodies, such as central banks and analytical teams like the OFR. To date, digital currencies relying on blockchain technology have lacked central bank backing. These currencies have operated as small-scale payments media rather than money supplies managed to achieve inflation or unemployment outcomes or to stabilize financial systems. Perhaps because of this, together with the absence of adjustments such as legal tender recognition, no blockchain currency has thus far grown big enough to present stability concerns. Nonetheless, central banks and others are watching this issue[42].

This section will address the intervention question first – this has already been discussed to some degree in prior sections. It will then turn to the more complex issue of data.

1. INTERVENTION MECHANISMS

In times of crisis, intervention can be necessary in a number of aspects of the financial system, whether to support liquidity, to prevent a run-away dynamic as in a flash crash, or to otherwise prevent the long-term harms that can result from a short-term breakdown. In this dynamic, payment services are a critical output of the financial system. Cryptocurrency innovators seek to augment or supplant the core players in the current system, but the systemic ramifications are unclear. For example, how would authorities or market participants restart payment systems that suffered from technical failures or loss of confidence? Similarly, how would blockchain technology participate in the unwinding of voided transactions after a trading halt as was imposed during the 2010 flash crash? As discussed in Section IV, if trades are recorded in a blockchain, market participants may require that the unwind protocol be incorporated in the same blockchain. Perhaps because of technical issues (e.g. a denial of service attack or a mutating computer virus), confidence in a market based upon the blockchain technology could erode. In a distributed system absent a guarantor, a governor, or a logical Samaritan, how will the system restart and rebuild confidence? Will there be the possibility for manual intervention or will the designers of the system insist on design that prevents intervention (even for noble reasons such as robustness to manipulation or protection of privacy, or other virtuous goals)?

While this concern exists for all aspects of business and regulation, it is particularly critical for financial stability in the context of resolution of firms, central counterparties, and financial market utilities. Should a critical node of the system fail, the existence of immutable blockchain transactions or contracts could hinder or thwart the ability of supervisors to resolve institutions, in much the same way as the ISDA master agreements' cross-default provisions hindered the ability to transition swaps from failing or failed counterparties[43].

2. DATA: EXTRACTION, EVALUATION AND ANALYSIS

Since 2008, there has been an increased attention to the cumulative, systemic effects of the individual actions in the financial markets. As discussed elsewhere, individual actions that are acceptable assumptions of risk or failures of payment in a single transaction can, if taken in the aggregate, create the equivalent of a heart attack in the system as a whole. Any attempt to understand, anticipate, and ameliorate this kind of effect must start with identifying and collecting the relevant data about transactions and markets. Recognizing patterns of concern and diagnosing impending failures all require getting information, separating out what is reliable, and putting it to work. Blockchain approaches both help and hinder these efforts.

Privacy and anonymity are entry-level concerns in this process. The decentralized ledger built into the first-generation implementations of the blockchain presupposes all-or-nothing transparency into the record of transactions. This is useful for establishing the consensus needed to maintain a valid blockchain ledger, but it creates problems when participants wish to record a transaction privately. Even in more general implementations, the distributed ledger must be open at least to validators (and potentially others), presenting questions about who has access to what information about transactions for supervisory or risk management purposes, under what circumstances, and in what format. Conversely, the transactors in the early stages of cryptocurrency use have often valued anonymity, probably from a range of concerns that span motivations from the innocent to the malign. The Bitcoin blockchain, for one, goes to great lengths to anonymize (or psuedonomize) the identity of transactors.

Although the Bitcoin anonymity can be useful in certain cases, for many financial transactions the unambiguous disclosure of the true identities of obligors and obligees matters very much. In short, the question is, how will blockchain implicate information flow and to whom? Second, does the law or its regulatory implementation permit the blockchain activity and leave available to supervisors or firms credible levers to implement policy adjustments given changing risks? Or will the governance framework chase away opportunities for improvements to the system, or foster regulatory arbitrage that could destabilize it? Third, can legal and governance systems designed to support the technology provide for self-help, recourse to judicial support, and intervention by private or public actors who can either provide support to the system during stress periods or resolve failed markets or utilities that rely upon the system? The law must be capable of enforcing rights established and represented in blockchain.

Another attribute of a distributed ledger – whether to support a currency, a payment system, a clearing or settlement regime, or secure contracting – is the absence of a central node for collection of information about the system or its actors or transactions. The many benefits of such an approach have been celebrated, including (potentially) anonymity, reduction of costs, avoidance of re-use (rehypothecation) of collateral and others[44]. Removal of a common ledger, however, could have consequences for both access to information and the quality of that information.

The BCBC, for example, builds in two forms of latency that are central to its process for building a consensus version of the truth into the distributed ledger. First, there is a mining latency for the brute-force calculations needed to establish the right to add a new block to the chain. It is theoretically necessary that this process be computationally costly – when signaling is costless, arbitrary nonsense (e.g., spam) or malicious misinformation can swamp the ledger. Currently, the BCBC mining costs periodically increase relative to reward, by intrinsic design (the "halving", a process where the mining incentive decreases by 50%). In theory, a different blockchain with higher reward, or a blockchain that touches a financial instrument worth considerably more (say, a trading blockchain that deals with transactions in the hundreds of millions or billions of dollars), could incentivize pursuit of fraudulent activity.

Second, there is a consensus latency needed for an adequate number of affirming votes to accumulate for a particular version of the blockchain to proceed as the consensus truth. Both forms of latency imply a temporal delay, which could create a tension, for example, if the BCBC were used to support high-frequency trading operations. Although early implementations, such as the BCBC, have strongly favored a decentralized ledger and distributed consensus in establishing the agreed version of the truth, the possibilities under alternative centralization assumptions have not yet been thoroughly explored, neither from a legal nor a technical perspective.

Alternatively, consider the example of the U.S. wholesale payment system, which handles trillions of dollars in transactions each day. Presently, access to information about that system, its operations, and the flow of dollars through it can be understood by surveying a relatively small number of clearing banks (such as the Federal Reserve Bank of New York) and financial market utilities (FMUs) that provide the settlement infrastructure[45]. A distributed ledger system could involve the same basic participants exchanging obligations, and thus result in the same basic access to information about the system as can be gathered now through the clearing banks and FMUs. As a result, the ability of supervisors and market participants to monitor the system could be left unchanged by the introduction of blockchain technology.

On the other hand, a decentralized ledger could diffuse this currently concentrated system — with many implications. First, information gathering about the system could be complicated, if not impossible, in a highly diffuse system, especially during rapidly changing, fluid situations, such as a market stress event. Capturing information about millions of disaggregate transactions and attributing them to central nodes or participants from perhaps thousands of servers would take computing power, time, and specialized tools that do not yet exist. This could also mean complications for efforts to identify failures and subsequently restart the system in the event of a cyber-attack such as a denial of service against multiple nodes of the distributed ledger.

Access to information about the distributed system could also be made difficult depending upon the cooperation of the nodes of the distributed ledger system, particularly if servers supporting mining activities are located in jurisdictions lacking suitable infrastructure (reliable power grids and communications or connectivity infrastructure) or legal frameworks (privacy and information sharing laws). Perhaps remote, another concern regarding ready access to information about or from a distributed system is the alignment of incentives to share information (or regulatory requirements to do so) by those which control the system. That is, if associated costs are such that a narrow group of well-funded miners effectively controls the system, what will be the mechanisms for assuring that information about or from the system is made available to competitors or authorities? It could require regulations that assure such cooperation and fair play.

Additionally, simple access to distributed information about the system does not imply the feasibility of integrating datasets from various venues and jurisdictions effectively. The technologies and standards for payment information exchange, particularly across borders, will require coordination. There are alternatives to coordinated information integration for purposes of monitoring, regulation, and resolution – an ad-hoc patchwork of local systems or a set of isolated silos – but any solution will present implementation challenges.

As noted above, anonymity or pseudonymity of transactors in a blockchain could raise other supervisory (and law enforcement) concerns. For example, given the traditional role of nodes in the system such as banks for filing Suspicious Activity Reports (SARs), information flow could be limited by a distributed ledger network. Anonymity was a low-level requirement for the Bitcoin blockchain, but it is not clear how crucial this feature is, or what other possibilities open up if this constraint is eased. Although law enforcement concerns are generally beyond the scope of this book, regulators will surely seek to have means to identify market actors and their actions both to protect its participants and to preserve trust in the system itself.

On the other hand, pre-trade anonymity is a crucial feature of many dealer markets, where knowledge of who is trading or whether they have come to buy or sell can, by itself, be sufficiently revelatory to drive trading away from the market altogether. The blockchain ledger would represent a new information source in these intricate environments, and the implications for existing microstructures are far from clear. It is not clear that a blockchain would necessarily disrupt existing relationships, nor is it clear whether such disruption would be good or bad, on net. One should acknowledge, however, that the potential for disruption exists, and stay attuned to its ramifications as innovations are introduced. For example, the possible loss of anonymity might drive trading away from central nodes of the system into bilateral markets, which in turn could have implications for firms' internal risk management systems, particularly if they lack the information necessary to monitor risk exposures.

This concern touches the regulatory system in several respects. Since 2002, the Sarbanes-Oxley law has required that corporate executives in the United States certify the adequacy of internal controls for risk management systems. Gathering the information necessary to meet this compliance requirement could be even more challenging in a distributed system if transactions are recorded and positions reflected on multiple, dynamic platforms. The costs of maintaining internal risk management systems that ingest information from distributed ledgers could prove high. A similar concern arises in the context of the stress testing of banks now required for compliance with the Dodd-Frank Act. Risk management systems may need retooling to comply with the requirements of the law, and supervisors – in this case the Federal Reserve and FDIC – will, likewise, need to adapt to identify the source of, and standards for, the data necessary to perform their supervisory functions.

Supervisors have invested significant effort to align reporting and transaction standards to improve the quality of information about the financial system. A good example is the creation of swaps data repositories, central counterparties, and swap execution facilities, where the OFR and other regulators are working to align data standards for entities, products, transactions, and myriad other data fields. As previously discussed, a possibly transformative application of blockchain technology would be for messaging, settling, clearing and reporting the transaction using a single decentralized ledger. Here again, blockchain technology is not a panacea, however. Without common standards to reflect the legal and economic terms of the transactions and their counterparties, the pre-crisis opacity overlaying our derivatives markets would persist, regardless of the promise of blockchain technology. What remains then are questions of who and how will these standards develop? Will competitive forces drive narrow, proprietary blockchain systems? Or will early steps be taken to avoid a disjoined collection of specific, one-off blockchain implementations that suffer from the kinds of classic collective action problems that have hamstrung financial markets for years?

Finally, blockchain technology presents a significant opportunity to improve on many aspects of our financial infrastructure. One critical area is access to information by appropriate authorities, and the ability to securely share that information. In making design decisions, technologists could consider the benefits of improving the ability of supervisors to supervise such that they can perform their critical role in overseeing orderly markets, protecting investors, testing the soundness of institutions at the core of the financial system, and building trust and confidence in our financial markets. Hopefully this will be an opportunity taken rather than a lost one.

VII. CONCLUSIONS AND STEPS FORWARD

We are only at the dawn of realizing the potential of disruptive financial technologies. The coming years will see new applications emerge, new kinds of organizations develop, and new consequences arise that will need to be dealt with by a diverse community of stakeholders.

The technological and application developments for financial innovation will inevitably be accompanied by developments in government rule-setting and oversight: in short, regulation. Some of this will involve applying existing rules and oversight structures; some will involve creating new provisions that will better fit the particular needs of a technologically-based application. In this chapter we have sought to provide a framework for imagining what this future interaction of financial innovations such as blockchain with government may look like, along with our admittedly speculative vision of some of the possible points of contact. We hope that this combined exercise can be a useful starting point for further deliberation and consideration as the process goes forward.

Our thinking so far has largely focused on the substance of the applicable rules. In closing, we also wish to speculate on the process by which they will be developed. We strongly urge technology advocates such as the blockchain user community to seek involvement, and in some cases partnership, with the various points of contact in government as this goes forward. For the most part, this engagement will lead to better outcomes. Modern regulatory process often invokes a model of multi-stakeholder dialog, with the goal of eliciting approaches that best serve the industry as well as the public and the needs of government itself. The technical complexity of blockchain applications makes this need for engagement even more critical.

A similar admonition can be aimed at governmental actors. As envisioned in such principals as those set out in Circular A-4, where possible, governmental intervention should consist of light-handed regulation, based on market and self-governing principles developed in consultation with those most affected.

Such a collaborative process can never be fully harmonious; there are simply too many diverging interests between and within the various classes of players. But it can nonetheless be far more productive than contentious processes, based on hostility, mutual suspicion and avoidance. We hope that this book can help to catalyze the next stages in the process.

The authors invite comment and feedback, and hope that this will not be the end of the discussion, but the beginning of a robust dialog about blockchain application, opportunity and policy.

CHAPTER 8

Future Directions:

Towards the Internet of Trusted Data

David Shrier, Alex Pentland

Thank you for joining us in our exploration of the frontiers of financial technology.

Of necessity, we left out several key Future Commerce topics — a deeper dive in artificial intelligence, an exploration of crowdfunding, applications of complex systems analysis to financial services, new forms of credit analytics, many more — and we hope to incorporate those into a future volume.

The Internet of Trusted Data

We are, at this moment, in the middle of a dramatic transformation from the "analog" world to the "digital" world. The trivial example of the commercial success of the game Pokemon Go hints at the barest edges of this.

The transformation of our current management of identity and of data is a foundational area for development. Identity is the root from which sprouts entry into the financial system, access to government services, and engagement with the health system. However, our systems of creating and managing identity are woefully behind the actual state of behavior in the world, and there is significant friction at the interface between analog and digital (anyone who has waited on line at a TSA security station has felt this).

A better system of identity engages harmoniously in dialog with a better system of data. Today's data systems have large "attack surfaces" making data breaches easier. Large-scale fraud, identity theft, and data theft are all too common, and a large number of people only have the most basic security tools to protect their personal information.

On 11 July 2016, the Massachusetts Institute of Technology Connection Science Initiative convened a workshop of industry and government leaders to recommend a new paradigm for identity and data, in response to the White House Commission on Cybersecurity, and separately discussions with the U.S. Secretary of Commerce Penny Pritzker and Andrus Ansip, the European Union's Vice President of the Single Digital Market.

If we create an Internet of Trusted Data where people can be ensured that their personal information—identification, health records and prescriptions, finances, and other data—is safe, secure, and accessible to only those who are authorized, then huge societal benefits can be unlocked.

However, trust must be earned by creating specific measures of transparency and accountability for securely managing such personal information shared between people and institutions. The potential benefits to be unlocked by the Internet of Trusted Data include almost everything from more secure financial transactions, improved access to personal healthcare information, and more efficient and effective government and private-sector services.

An Internet of Trusted Data includes:

- **Robust Digital Identity**. Identity, whether personal or organizational, is the key that unlocks all other data and data sharing functions. Digital Identity includes not only having unique and unforgeable credentials that work everywhere, but also the ability to access all the data linked to your identity and the ability to control the "persona" that you present in different situations. To accomplish this there needs to be a kind of "internet of identity" to genuinely enable all other sharing functions. There are a number of technological, social and political challenges to overcome to make this a reality.

- **Distributed Internet Trust Authorities.** We have repeatedly seen that centralized system administration can be the weakest link in cybersecurity, enabling both insiders and opponents to destroy our system security with a single exploit. The most practical solution to this problem is to have authority distributed among many trusted actors, so that compromise of one or even a few authorities does not destroy the system security consensus.

- **Distributed safe computation.** Our critical systems will suffer increasing rates of damage and compromise unless we move decisively toward pervasive use of data minimization, more encryption and distributed computation. We need to adopt an inherently more robust approach that is, for instance, built on distributed consensus algorithms for data sharing and usage permissions, and can therefore track and can audit data provenance. It is also critical that such a solution have the maximum encryption protection. MIT Enigma and OPAL ("Open Algorithms") are steps toward this end.

- **Universal Access.** The advantages of secure digital infrastructure are diminished without universal access. The United Nations has set a goal of having all humans on the planet gain access to services and support through biometric identification by 2030. Privacy and security concerns that arise from such a system are addressed, in part, by the other dimensions of the Internet of Trusted Data outlined above, but require further discussion and elaboration before a practical, and socially viable, system emerges.

In Conclusion

The frontiers of financial technology are constantly changing. Part of why we find it such an exciting area is the potential for the unexpected, such as the use of animal behavioral models to help a bank better manage consumer credit risk.

Most importantly, we learn from the thousands of students who take our classes to develop new ventures. Our students serve as our inspiration, and we look forward to the global change they will drive through their innovations.

We hope this volume will inspire you in shaping your own cutting edge financial technology idea, and that we someday will be writing about the impact you have had on the world.

David Shrier, Alex Pentland
Cambridge, MA
August 2016

Participants in MIT's 11 July 2016 workshop on the Internet of Trusted Data included:

- Alex Pentland (Professor, MIT)
- Irving Wladawsky-Berger (MIT Connection Science Fellow)
- David Shrier (Managing Director, MIT Connection Science)
- Jerry Cuomo (IBM Fellow and Vice President Blockchain Technologies)
- Steve Davis (Senior Consultant, Payments Innovation, MasterCard)
- Michael Frank (Program Director; Blockchain Technologies, IBM)
- Thomas Hardjono (Chief Technology Officer, MIT Connection Science)
- Guerney Hunt (Research Staff Member, IBM)
- Cameron Kerry (former General Counsel and Acting Secretary, U.S. Department of Commerce, Visiting Scholar MIT and Brookings Institute)
- Mark O'Riley (Office of the General Counsel, Government and Regulatory Affair- Technology Policy, IBM)
- Chris Parsons (Vice President Big Data Strategy and Business Development, AT&T)
- Gari Singh (Distinguished Engineer and Blockchain CTO, IBM)
- Anne Shere Wallwork (Senior Counselor for Strategic Policy, Office of Terrorist Financing and Financial Crimes, U.S. Department of the Treasury)
- Rod Walton (VP Qualcomm)
- Irida Xheneti (Entrepreneur in Residence, MIT Connection Science)

References

CHAPTER 1: 5TH HORIZON OF NETWORKED INNOVATION

[1] MIT personal conversations with CEOs of over 60 leading financial services and technology companies, Davos Switzerland, January 2016.

[2] Prediction: $10 Billion Will Be Invested in Blockchain Projects in 2016 http://coinjournal.net/prediction-10-billion-will-be-invested-in-blockchain-startups-in-2016/

[3] Google Webtrends, accessed 19 March 2016.

[4] Santander InnoVentures, Oliver Wyman, Anthemis Group, "The FinTech 2.0 Paper" (2015).

[5] "The socio-economic impact of interoperable electronic health record (EHR) and ePrescribing systems in Europe and beyond" (2009) European Commission Information Society and Media Directorate.

[6] "US Health Care Costs Surge to 17 Percent of GDP", The Fiscal Times (2015) http://www.thefiscaltimes.com/2015/12/03/Federal-Health-Care-Costs-Surge-17-Percent-GDP

[7] Clippinger J, Bollier D *From Bitcoin to Burning Man and Beyond* (2015).

[8] MIT Enigma Project: https://enigma.media.mit.edu

[9] T. Hardjono, ChainAnchor: Cloud-Based Commissioning of Constrained Devices using Permissioned Blockchains, Proceedings of ACM IoT Privacy, Trust and Security 2016.

[10] Others have pointed out earlier antecedents to blockchain - http://www.ofnumbers.com/2015/07/09/a-blockchain-with-emphasis-on-the-a/

[11] http://www.economist.com/blogs/economist-explains/2015/01/economist-explains-11 accessed May 2016.

[12] Personal conversation between a CTO of a blockchain company and the authors, March 2016.

[13] /u/throw_awa5 posted 27 April 2016 https://www.reddit.com/r/Bitcoin/comments/4givro/upcoming_ama_mit_connection_science_team_will/d2jig1r accessed 30 April 2016.

[14] Maras M (2016) "R3 Consortium's Blockchain Initiative: What Makes Corda Different?" Cryptocoin News https://www.cryptocoinsnews.com/r3-consortiums-blockchain-initiative-what-makes-corda-different/

[15] Metz C (2016) "The Plan to Unite Bitcoin With All Other Online Currencies" Wired. http://www.wired.com/2016/01/project-aims-to-unite-bitcoin-with-other-online-currencies/

[16] Greenberg A. (2015) "MIT's Bitcoin-Inspired 'Enigma' Lets Computers Mine Encrypted Data" WIRED https://www.wired.com/2015/06/mits-bitcoin-inspired-enigma-lets-computers-mine-encrypted-data/

CHAPTER 2: TRANSACTIONS, MARKETS & MARKETPLACES

[1] Santander InnoVentures, Oliver Wyman, Anthemis Group (2015) "The Fintech 2.0 Paper: rebooting financial services"

[2] Stein, P (2015) "5 steps to closing the $2 trillion credit gap" World Economic Forum https://www.weforum.org/agenda/2015/10/5-steps-to-closing-the-2-trillion-credit-gap/

[3] The World Bank. Enterprise Surveys. (http://www.enterprisesurveys.org). 2010-2016.

[4] Love, Inessa, Sandeep Singh, and Maria Soledad Martínez Pería. "Collateral Registries for Movable Assets: Does Their Introduction Spur Firms' Access to Bank Finance?" January 2013. http://www.ifc.org/wps/wcm/connect/8891c280415edb709ba3bb9e78015671/Collateral+Registries+for+Movable+Assets++Does+Their+Introduction+Spu+Firms+Access+to+Bank+Finance.pdf?MOD=AJPERES.

[5] International Finance Corporation. Secured Transactions and Collateral Registries (http://www.ifc.org/wps/wcm/connect/793e79804ac10fff9ea69e4220e715ad/Secured+Transactions+and+Collateral+Registries+Brochure-English.pdf?MOD=AJPERES).

[6] Nash, Kim S. "Blockchain: Catalyst for Massive Change Across Industries." Wall Street Journal. February 2, 2016.
http://blogs.wsj.com/cio/2016/02/02/blockchain-catalyst-for-massive-change-across-industries/.

[7] http://www.iacc.org/resources/about/statistics accessed 07 May 2016.

[8] Bloomberg News. "China Fake Invoice Evidence Mounts as HK Figures Diverge." Bloomberg. October 27, 2014.
http://www.bloomberg.com/news/articles/2014-10-27/china-fake-invoice-evidence-mounts-as-hong-kong-figures-diverge.

[9] UK Government Chief Scientific Advisor. "Distributed Ledger Technology: beyond Blockchain." Government Office for Science. 2016

[10] "Collateral Management – Unlocking the Potential in Collateral." Accenture and Clearstream, 2011.

[11] Metz, Cade. "Coinbase Is Out to Build Payments Right Into Browsers." Wired. Nov. 13, 2015. http://www.wired.com/2015/11/coinbase-is-bringing-back-the-webs-long-lost-payment-code/

[12] W3C. "Common Markup for micropayment per-fee-links" Aug. 25, 1999. https://www.w3.org/TR/WD-Micropayment-Markup/#origin-goals

[13] Kaufman, Stacy, Ramani, Abhinav, Luciano, Dave, Zou, Long and Fosco, James. "Micropayments: A Viable Business Model?" Stanford University. June 2, 2011. http://cs.stanford.edu/people/eroberts/courses/cs181/projects/2010-11/MicropaymentsAndTheNet/index.html.

[14] Lebleu, G. "Building Gift Cards 2.0 on the Blockchain an overview." June 16th, 2015. https://medium.com/@giyom/building-gift-cards-2-0-on-the-block-chain-3ae9e7cf4152#.1zeoabmly.

[15] Oliver Wyman and Euroclear. "Blockchain in Capital Markets: the prize and the journey." Feb. 2016.

[16] Levine, Matt. "Banks Forgot Who Was Supposed to Own Dell Shares." Bloomberg View. Jul. 14th, 2015. http://www.bloombergview.com/articles/2015-07-14/banks-forgot-who-was-supposed-to-own-dell-shares.

[17] Vigna, Paul. "Nasdaq's Blockchain-Based Securities Platform Records First Transaction." Wall Street Journal. Dec 20th, 2015. http://blogs.wsj.com/moneybeat/2015/12/30/nas-daqs-blockchain-based-securities-platform-records-first-transaction/.

[18] "The Fintech 2.0 Paper: rebooting financial services." Santander InnoVentures, Oliver Wyman and Anthemis Group. 2016. http://santanderinnoventures.com/wp-content/up-loads/2015/06/The-Fintech-2-0-Paper.pdf.

[19] DeRose, Chris. "Smart Contracts are the Future of Blockchain." Jan. 11th, 2016. http://www.paymentssource.com/news/paythink/smart-contracts-are-the-future-of-block-chain-3023206-1.html

[20] Schanz Kai-Uwe and Wang S, "The Global Insurance Protection Gap Assessment and Recommendations" (2014), The Geneva Association. https://www.genevaassociation.org/media/909569/ga2014-the_global_insurance_protection_gap.pdf

[21] http://blogs.wsj.com/cio/2016/02/02/blockchain-catalyst-for-massive-change-across-in-dustries/

[22] Green M (2014) "Zero Knowledge Proofs: an illustrated primer" http://blog.cryptography-engineering.com/2014/11/zero-knowledge-proofs-illustrated-primer.html

[23] Kentouris, C (2015) "US T+2 Settlement: The Long Journey Officially Begins" FinOps Re-port. http://finops.co/investments/us-t2-settlement-the-long-journey-officially-begins/

[24] CFTC. "CFTC Tackles the What Ifs of Blockchain."

[25] Shin L "How Will Bitcoin Technology Go Mainstream? An Analysis Of 5 Strategies" (2016) Forbes http://www.forbes.com/sites/laurashin/2016/01/26/how-will-bitcoin-technolo-gy-go-mainstream-an-analysis-of-5-strategies/#47767db63c31

CHAPTER 3: INFRASTRUCTURE (IDENTITY, DATA SECURITY)

[1] Jonathan Woetzel et al., "Preparing for China's Urban Billion" (McKinsey Global Institute, March 2009),

http:// www.mckinsey.com/ insights/ urbanization/ preparing_for_urban_billion_in_china.

[2] ShoCard. 2015. Homepage. Accessed 2 21, 2016. http://www.shocard.com.

[3] Uniquid. n.d. Homepage. Accessed 2 21, 2016. http://www.uniquid.co.

[4] KPMG. 2014. Global Anti-Money Laundering Survey 2014. KPMG International Co-operative.

[5] ascribe GmbH. 2016. ascribe for Artists & Creators. Accessed 2 21, 2016. http://www.ascribe.io.

[6] Blockverify. n.d. Homepage. Accessed 2 21, 2016. www.blockverify.io.

[7] The Economist. 2015. The great chain of being sure about things. 10 31. Accessed 2 21, 2017. http://www.economist.com/news/briefing/21677228-technology-behind-bitcoin-lets-people-who-do-not-know-or-trust-each-other-build-dependable.

[8] Sanger DE and E Schmitt "nowden Used Low-Cost Tool to Best N.S.A." *New York Times*, http://www.nytimes.com/2014/02/09/us/snowden-used-low-cost-tool-to-best-nsa.html?_r=0.

[9] Zyskin, Guy, Oz Nathan, and Alex 'Sandy' Pentland. n.d. "Enigma: Decentralized Computation Platform with Guaranteed Security." White paper.

[10] *Ibid.*

[11] *Ibid.*

[12] Storj. 2016. Homepage. Accessed 2 21, 2016. http://www.storj.io.

[13] Factom. 2014. Healthnautica, Factom announce partnership. 4 23. Accessed 22 21, 2016. http://www.factom.com/healthnautica-factom-announce-partnership/.

[14] Meglena Kuneva, European Consumer Commissioner, "Keynote Speech," in Roundtable on Online Data Collection, Targeting and Profiling, March 31, 2009, http:// europa.eu/ rapid/ press-release_SPEECH-09-156_en.htm

[15] Kim Gittleson, "How Big Data Is Changing The Cost Of Insurance," BBC News, November 14, 2013, http:// www.bbc.co.uk/ news/ business-24941415.

[16] Aniko Hannak, Piotr Sapiezynski, Kakhki Arash Molavi, Balachander Krishnamurthy, David Lazer, Alan Mislove, and Christo Wilson, "Measuring Personalization of Web Search," in Proc. 22nd International Conference on World Wide Web (WWW 2013), 527–538

[17] Pentland A, "Reality Mining of Mobile Communications." (2009) *Social Computing and Behavioral Modeling.*

[18] Madan A, Cebrian M, Lazer D, Pentland A, "Social Sensing for Epidemiological Behavior Change," in Proc. 12th ACM International Conference on Ubiquitous Computing

(Ubicomp 2010), 291– 300; Pentland et al. "Using Reality Mining to Improve Public Health and Medicine."

[19] Wei Pan, Gourab Ghoshal, Coco Krumme, Manuel Cebrian, and Alex Pentland, "Urban Characteristics Attributable to Density-Driven Tie Formation," Nature Communications 4 (2013): article 1961.

[20] Lev Grossman, "Iran Protests: Twitter, the Medium of the Movement," Time Magazine, June 17, 2009; Ellen Barry, "Protests in Moldova Explode, with Help of Twitter," The New York Times, April 8, 2009.

[21] "Directive 95/ 46/ EC of the European Parliament and of the Council of 24 October 1995 on the Protection of Individuals with Regard to the Processing of Personal Data and on the Free Movement of Such Data," Official Journal L281 (November 23, 1995): 31– 50.

[22] World Economic Forum, "Personal Data: The Emergence of a New Asset Class," January 2011,
http:// www.weforum.org/ reports/ personal-data-emergence-new-asset-class.

[23] Ibid.

[24] Ibid.

[25] Lima A, De Domenico M, Pejovic V, Musolesi M, "Exploiting Cellular Data for Disease Containment and Information Campaign Strategies in Country-Wide Epidemics," School of Computer Science Technical Report CSR-13-01, University of Birmingham, May 2013.

[26] Narayanan A, Shmatikov V, "Robust De-Anonymization of Large Sparse Datasets," in Proc. 2008 IEEE Symposium on Security and Privacy (SP), 111– 125.

[27] Latanya Sweeney, "Simple Demographics Often Identify People Uniquely," Data Privacy Working Paper 3, Carnegie Mellon University, Pittsburgh, 2000.

[28] de Montjoye Y, Wang A, Pentland A, "On the Trusted Use of Large-Scale Personal Data," IEEE Data Engineering Bulletin 35, no. 4 (2012): 5– 8.

[29] Song C, Qu Z, Blumm N, Barabasi A, "Limits of Predictability in Human Mobility," Science 327 (2010): 1018– 1021.

[30] Pentland A, Lazer D, Brewer D, Heibeck T, "Using Reality Mining to Improve Public Health and Medicine." Stud Health Technol Inform. (2009) 149:93-102.

[31] Tacconi D, Mayora O, Lukowicz P, Arnrich B, Setz C, Troster G, Haring C, "Activity and Emotion Recognition to Support Early Diagnosis of Psychiatric Diseases," in Proc. 2nd International ICST Conference on Pervasive Computing Technologies for Healthcare, 100– 102.

[32] World Economic Forum, "Personal Data."

[33] The White House, "National Strategy for Trusted Identities in Cyberspace: Enhancing Online Choice, Efficiency, Security, and Privacy," Washington, DC, April 2011, http://www.whitehouse.gov/sites/default/files/rss_viewer/NSTICstrategy_041511.pdf

CHAPTER 4: MOBILE MONEY & PAYMENTS

[1] British Museum http://www.britishmuseum.org/explore/themes/money/the_origins_of_coinage.aspx

[2] Schmandt-Besserat, D (2008) "Two Precursors of Writing: Plain and Complex Tokens" http://en.finaly.org/index.php/Two_precursors_of_writing:_plain_and_complex_tokens

[3] Desan C (2015) "Making Money: Coin, Currency and the Coming of Capitalism" Oxford University Press.

[4] Commission of the European Communities. EU Directive Proposal, 9.10.2008 http://ec.europa.eu/internal_market/payments/docs/emoney/com_2008_627_en.pdf

[5] GSMA and MMU. "Mobile Money Definitions." July 2010. http://www.gsma.com/mobilefordevelopment/wp-content/uploads/2012/06/mobilemoneydefinitionsnomarks56.pdf

[6] GSMA and MMU. "State of the Industry: Results from the 2012 Global Mobile Money Adoption Survey." http://www.gsma.com/mobilefordevelopment/wp-content/uploads/2013/02/MMU_State_of_industry.pdf

[7] CGAP, GSMA, and McKinsey & Company "Mobile Money Market Sizing Study." CGAP Brief. http://www.gsma.com/mobilefordevelopment/wp-content/uploads/2012/06/br_mobile_money_philippines_d_30.pdf.

[8] CGAP. "Mobile Money: 10 Things You Need to Know." Dec. 30, 2013. http://www.cgap.org/blog/mobile-money-10-things-you-need-know

[9] Aristotle. "Politics." Translated by Benjamin Jowett. Cambridge: MIT. http://classics.mit.edu/Aristotle/politics.1.one.html.

[10] Evans, David Sparks and Schmalensee, Richard. "Paying with Plastic: The Digital Revolution in Buying and Borrowing." MIT Press: 1 January 2005 ISBN 026255058X.

[11] Burn-Callander, Rebecca. "The History of Money: From Barter to Bitcoin." The Telegraph, October 20, 2014. http://www.telegraph.co.uk/finance/businessclub/money/11174013/The-history-of-money-from-barter-to-bitcoin.html.

[12] Hammonds, Keith. "Pay As You Go." Fast Company, October 31, 2001. http://www.fastcompany.com/44023/pay-you-go.

[13] Nakomoto, S (2008) "Bitcoin: A Peer-to-Peer Electronic Cash System". http://www.cryptovest.co.uk/resources/Bitcoin%20paper%20Original.pdf

[14] Long, C (2016) "Central Banks Can't Ignore Blockchain's Obvious Lure" American Banker June 10, 2016 http://www.americanbanker.com/bankthink/central-banks-cant-ignore-blockchains-obvious-lure-1081428-1.html

[15] UK Government Office for Science (2016) "Distributed Ledger Technology: beyond block chain" https://www.gov.uk/government/uploads/system/uploads/attachment_data/

file/492972/gs-16-1-distributed-ledger-technology.pdf

[16] Rizzo P (2016) "Japan Enacts Regulation for Digital Currency Exchanges" Coindesk. com May 25, 2016 http://www.coindesk.com/japan-enacts-regulation-digital-currency-exchanges/

[17] O'Ham T (2016) "Vatican Slated as First State Adopters of Cryptocurrency" April 1, 2016 http://bitcoinist.net/vatican-adop-cryptocurrency/

[18] "Bitt Launches the Blockchain Barbadian Digital Dollar" February 25, 2016 Cryptocoin News https://www.cryptocoinsnews.com/bitt-launches-the-blockchain-barbadian-digital-dollar/

[19] MasterCard, Kahtan, M. "New MasterCard Advisors Study on Contactless Payments Shows Almost 30% Lift in Total Spend Within First Year of Adoption." 2012. http://newsroom.mastercard.com/press-releases/new-mastercard-advisors-study-on-contactless-payments-shows-almost-30-lift-in-total-spend-within-first-year-of-adoption/.

[20] Nazareno, N. Smart Communications, 2008. Presentation at GSMA Mobile Money Summit in Cairo, May 14.

[21] Runde, D. "M-Pesa And The Rise Of The Global Mobile Money Market." Forbes, August 12, 2015. http://www.forbes.com/sites/danielrunde/2015/08/12/m-pesa-and-the-rise-of-the-global-mobile-money-market/#b7fd90b23f5d

[22] Parrin, A. "Kenya's No.1 mobile network is battling one of the country's top banks for mobile money's future." Quartz Africa, June 19, 2015. http://qz.com/430666/kenyas-no-1-mobile-network-is-battling-one-of-the-countrys-top-banks-for-mobile-moneys-future/

[23] World Bank Group. Global Findex Database. 2014.

[24] Cobert, B; Helms, B; Parker, D and McKinsey & Company. "Mobile money: Getting to scale in emerging markets." May 2012. http://www.mckinsey.com/industries/social-sector/our-insights/mobile-money-getting-to-scale-in-emerging-markets.

[25] di Castri, S. "A conversation with Professor Njuguna Ndung'u, Governor of the Central Bank of Kenya, on the critical policy issues around mobile money." GSMA Blog, 2013. http://www.gsma.com/mobilefordevelopment/a-conversation-with-professor-njuguna-ndungu-governor-of-the-central-bank-of-kenya-on-the-critical-policy-issues-around-mobile-money.

[26] Singh VK, Bozkaya B & Pentland A. "Money Walks: Implicit Mobility Behavior and Financial Well-Being". 2015.

[27] Warman, Yael. "How Mobile Moves." Forex Crunch. January 18, 2016. Accessed April 04, 2016. https://www.forexcrunch.com/how-mobile-moves/.

[28] Stock Trading Warrior. "History of Online Stock Trading." Stock Trading Warrior. Accessed April 04, 2016. http://www.stock-trading-warrior.com/History-of-Online-Stock-Trading.html.

[29] Be Businessed. "History of Online Stock Trading." Be Businessed. 2015. Accessed April 04, 2016. http://bebusinessed.com/history/history-of-online-stock-trading/.

[30] CDW Financial Insights. "The Latest Trends in Mobile Trading - FinTalk." FinTalk: Financial IT Insights. February 01, 2016. Accessed April 04, 2016. http://fintalk.cdw.com/2016/02/01/mobile-fin-news/.

[31] Carey, Theresa W. "Barron's 2015 Best Online Broker Ranking." Barron's 2015 Ranking of Online Brokers. March 7, 2015. Accessed April 04, 2016. http://www.barrons.com/articles/barrons-2015-ranking-of-online-brokers-1425705011.

[32] Estimize. Accessed April 04, 2016. https://www.estimize.com/.

[33] Vetr.com. Accessed April 04, 2016. https://www.vetr.com/.

[34] Motif Investing. "Motif - An Online Brokerage Built Around You." Motif. Accessed April 04, 2016. http://www.motifinvesting.com/.

[35] "Schwab Reports Monthly Activity Highlights" May 13, 2016 http://pressroom.aboutschwab.com/press-release/corporate-and-financial-news/schwab-reports-monthly-activity-highlights-64

[36] "ETrade Financial Corporation Reports Monthly Activity for April 2016" May 13, 2016. https://about.etrade.com/releasedetail.cfm?ReleaseID=970888

[37] TD Ameritrade. Accessed June 2016 (as of 3/31/2016 data) http://www.amtd.com/investor-relations/by-the-numbers/default.aspx

[38] Robinhood. "How Robinhood Makes Money." Robinhood Help Center. November 19, 2015. Accessed April 04, 2016. https://support.robinhood.com/hc/en-us/articles/202853769-How-does-Robinhood-make-money-.

[39] Yochim, Dayana. "Best Online Brokers for Free Trading - NerdWallet." NerdWallet. March 15, 2016. Accessed April 04, 2016. https://www.nerdwallet.com/blog/investing/free-stock-trading/.

[40] Shu C (2015) "FeeX, Which IDs Hidden Fees In Financial Products, Scores $2.75M In Fresh Funding" September 8, 2015 http://techcrunch.com/2015/09/08/feex-newfunding/

[41] Sharf S (2015) "BlackRock To Buy FutureAdvisor, Signaling Robo-Advice Is Here To Stay" Forbes, August 26, 2015 http://www.forbes.com/sites/samanthasharf/2015/08/26/blackrock-to-buy-futureadvisor-signaling-robo-advice-is-here-to-stay/#1901c3fe2294

[42] Bank of America. "Transfers". 2016. Accessed June 13, 2016 http://promo.bankofamerica.com/onlinepayments1/transfers.html

[43] PYMNTS. "Throwback Thrusday: PayPal's Biggest Days in History". July 2, 2015. Accessed June 13, 2016. http://www.pymnts.com/in-depth/2015/throwback-thursday-paypals-biggest-days-in-history/

[44] "PayPal About - Home." PayPal About - Home. Accessed May 05, 2016. https://www.paypal.com/us/webapps/mpp/about.

[45] Rao, Leena, Sarah Perez, and Ingrid Lunden. "EBay's PayPal Acquires Payments Gateway Braintree For $800M In Cash." TechCrunch. September 26, 2013. Accessed May 05, 2016.

[46] Russell, Jon. "Messaging App WeChat Is Becoming a Mobile Payment Giant in China." TechCrunch. March 17, 2016. Accessed May 05, 2016. http://techcrunch.com/2016/03/17/messaging-app-wechat-is-becoming-a-mobile-payment-giant-in-china/.

[47] Constine, Josh. "Facebook Introduces Free Friend-To-Friend Payments Through Messages." TechCrunch. March 17, 2015. Accessed May 05, 2016. http://techcrunch.com/2015/03/17/facebook-pay/.

[48] "Google Wallet." Google Wallet. Accessed May 05, 2016. https://www.google.com/wallet/faq/.

[49] Russell, Jon. "Messaging App WeChat Is Becoming a Mobile Payment Giant in China." TechCrunch. March 17, 2016. Accessed May 05, 2016. http://techcrunch.com/2016/03/17/messaging-app-wechat-is-becoming-a-mobile-payment-giant-in-china/.

[50] Rao, Leena. "You Will Soon Be Able to Shop Using Venmo." You Will Soon Be Able to Shop Using Venmo Comments. October 28, 2015. Accessed May 05, 2016. http://fortune.com/2015/10/28/venmo-paypal-merchants/.

[51] World Bank. Migration and Remittances Factbook 2016. Report. Advance ed. World Bank Group, 2016.

[52] World Bank. Migration and Remittances Factbook 2016. Report. Advance ed. World Bank Group, 2016.

[53] Let's Talk Payments. "FinTech Is Pushing Banks out of the Remittance Business." Let's Talk Payments. February 10, 2016. Accessed April 11, 2016. http://letstalkpayments.com/fintech-is-pushing-banks-out-of-the-remittance-business/.

[54] Life.SREDA, INSEAD, Deloitte. "Money of The Future." Money of the Future 2015. Accessed April 11, 2016. http://www.lifesreda.com/MoneyOfTheFuture_2016_eng.pdf.

[55] Rumayor, Inigo. "5 Things We Got Wrong In FinTech." Regalii. May 26, 2015. Accessed April 11, 2016. https://www.regalii.com/blog/5-things-we-got-wrong-in-fintech.

[56] Let's Talk Payments. "FinTech Is Pushing Banks out of the Remittance Business." Let's Talk Payments. February 10, 2016. Accessed April 11, 2016. http://letstalkpayments.com/fintech-is-pushing-banks-out-of-the-remittance-business/.

[57] Rumayor, Inigo. "5 Things We Got Wrong In FinTech." Regalii. May 26, 2015. Accessed April 11, 2016. https://www.regalii.com/blog/5-things-we-got-wrong-in-fintech.

[58] Let's Talk Payments. "FinTech Is Pushing Banks out of the Remittance Business." Let's Talk Payments. February 10, 2016. Accessed April 11, 2016. http://letstalkpayments.com/fintech-is-pushing-banks-out-of-the-remittance-business/.

[59] Sendwave. "Sendwave - Send Money to Africa." Sendwave - Send Money to Africa. Accessed April 11, 2016. https://www.sendwave.com/.

[60] Life.SREDA, INSEAD, Deloitte. "Money of The Future." Money of the Future 2015. Accessed April 11, 2016. http://www.lifesreda.com/MoneyOfTheFuture_2016_eng.pdf.

[61] BI Intelligence. "Fintech could be bigger than ATMs, PayPal and Bitcoin combined." Business Insider. April 12, 2016. Accessed June 13, 2016. http://www.businessinsider.com/fintech-ecosystem-financial-technology-research-and-business-opportunities-2016-2

[62] Griffithe, Ken. "A Quick history of Cryptocurrencies BBTC – Before Bitcoin." Bitcoin Magazine. April 16, 2014. Accessed June 13, 2016. https://bitcoinmagazine.com/articles/quick-history-cryptocurrencies-bbtc-bitcoin-1397682630

[63] Torpey, Kyle. "Prediction: $10 Billion Will Be Invested in Blockchain Projects in 2016". Coin Journal. January 22, 2016. Accessed June 13, 2016. http://coinjournal.net/prediction-10-billion-will-be-invested-in-blockchain-startups-in-2016/

[64] The Economist, Airtime is money, January 2013

[65] Gilman, Lara. "What is the future of mobile money?" World Economic Forum. August 25, 2016. Accessed June 13, 2016. https://www.weforum.org/agenda/2015/08/what-is-the-future-of-mobile-money/

[66] GSMA (2015) "The Mobile Economy Sub-Saharan Africa" https://www.gsmaintelligence.com/research/?file=721eb3d4b80a36451202d0473b3c4a63&download

CHAPTER 5: PREDICTION MARKETS

[1] Galton, Francis. (1907) "Vox Populi." Nature 75, no. 1949 (March 7, 1907): 450-51.

[2] Ibid.

[3] ibid.

[4] Galton, Francis. (1907) "The Ballot Box." Nature 75, no. 1952 (March 28, 1907): 509-10. Accessed May 24, 2016. http://galton.org/cgi-bin/searchImages/galton/search/essays/pages/galton-1907-ballot-box_1.htm.

5 Galton, Francis. "Vox Populi." Nature 75, no. 1949 (March 7, 1907): 450-51.

[6] Graefe, Andreas. (2008) "Political Markets". In SAGE Handbook of Electoral Behavior, edited by Kai Alzheimer and Jocelyn Evans. SAGE Publications.

[7] Snowberg, Erik, Justin Wolfers, and Eric Zitzewitz. (2013) "Prediction Markets for Economic Forecasting." In Handbook of Economic Forecasting, edited by Graham Elliot and Allan Timmermann. Vol. 2. North-Holland.

[8] Henry B. Tippie College of Business. (2016) "What Is the IEM? - Iowa Electronic Markets." Iowa Electronic Markets. Accessed May 25, 2016. http://tippie.uiowa.edu/iem/media/summary.html.

[9] PredictIt. (2016) "PredictIt - Markets - World." https://www.predictit.org/Browse/Category/4/World.

[10] CME Group. (2016) "Timeline of CME Achievements." CME Group: How the World Advances. Accessed May 25, 2016. http://www.cmegroup.com/company/history/timeline-of-achievements.html.

[11] Roll, Richard. (1984) "Orange Juice and Weather." The American Economic Review 74, no. 5 (December 1984): 861-80.

[12] Snowberg, Erik, Justin Wolfers, and Eric Zitzewitz. (2013) "Prediction Markets for Economic Forecasting." In Handbook of Economic Forecasting, edited by Graham Elliott and Allan Timmerman, 689-1324. Vol. 2, Part B. Elsevier.

[13] Ibid.

[14] Metz, Cade. (2016) "Google's AI Wins Fifth And Final Game Against Go Genius Lee Sedol." Wired.com. March 15, 2016. Accessed May 25, 2016. http://www.wired.com/2016/03/googles-ai-wins-fifth-final-game-go-genius-lee-sedol/.

[15] Thompson, Clive. (2013) "Excerpt of Smarter Than You Think." Smarter Than You Think. Accessed May 25, 2016. http://smarterthanyouthink.net/excerpt/.

[16] Gartner. "Gartner Hype Cycle." Hype Cycle Research Methodology. Accessed May 27, 2016. http://www.gartner.com/technology/research/methodologies/hype-cycle.jsp.

[17] ibid.

[18] Polgreen, Philip M., Forrest D. Nelson, and George R. Neumann. (2006) "Use of Prediction Markets to Forecast Infectious Disease Activity." Clinical Infectious Diseases 44, no. 2

(December 14, 2006): 272-79. http://cid.oxfordjournals.org/content/44/2/272.full.pdf html.

[19] Ibid.

[20] Ledbetter, James. (2016) "The Fizz-dom of Crowds." Slate.com. April 16, 2016. Accessed May 22, 2016. http://www.slate.com/articles/news_and_politics/hey_wait_a_minute/2008/04/the_fizzdom_of_crowds.html

[21] Leonhardt, David. (2008) "Looking for Sure Political Bets at Online Prediction Market." The New York Times. February 13, 2008. Accessed May 25, 2016. http://www.nytimes.com/2008/02/13/business/13leonhardt.html.

[22] Rice, Andrew. (2014) "The Fall Of Intrade And The Business Of Betting On Real Life." BuzzFeed. February 20, 2014. Accessed May 27, 2016. https://www.buzzfeed.com/andrewrice/the-fall-of-intrade-and-the-business-of-betting-on-real-life?utm_term=.nqmaQw1Na#.dkKLBrjAL.

[23] ibid.

[24] Lalley, Steven P. (2015) "Quadratic Voting." Social Science Research Network, December 22, 2015. doi:http://dx.doi.org/10.2139/ssrn.2003531.

[25] "Interview with CEO of Vetr, Michael Vien." Telephone interview by authors. June 15, 2016.

[26] "Interview with Founder of Framed Data, Thomson Nguyen." Telephone interview by authors. March 17, 2016.

[27] "Interview with Andrew Lo", In-person interview, March 2016.

[28] Metz, Cade. (2016) "The Rise of the Artificially Intelligent Hedge Fund." Wired, January 25th, 2016. http://www.wired.com/2016/01/the-rise-of-the-artificially-intelligent-hedge-fund/.

[29] "Interview with Chief Scientist and Co-founder of Sentient, Babak Adjodat." Telephone interview by authors. March 14, 2016.

[30] Pentland A. (2013) "Beyond the Echo Chamber" Harvard Business Review https://hbr.org/2013/11/beyond-the-echo-chamber

[31] "Interview with Founder of Numerai, Richard Craib." Telephone interview by authors. March 14, 2016.

[32] Pentland, Alex. (2013) "Beyond the Echo Chamber." Harvard Business Review, November 2013. https://hbr.org/2013/11/beyond-the-echo-chamber.

[33] Rizzo, Pete. (2015) "Augur Bets on Bright Future for Blockchain Prediction Markets." CoinDesk, March 1, 2015. http://www.coindesk.com/augur-future-blockchain-prediction-market/.

[34] Parker, Luke. (2015) "The Era Of Prediction Markets Is At Hand." BraveNewCoin, June 3rd, 2015. http://bravenewcoin.com/news/the-era-of-prediction-markets-is-at-hand/.

CHAPTER 6: DIGITAL BANKING MANIFESTO

[1] A. Lipton (2016), "Modern monetary circuit theory" IJTAF. This paper provides detail explanation of how money is created and destroyed by the banking system as a whole and by individual banks. It also shows that individual banks become naturally interconnected in the process.

[2] Bureau of Labor Statistics (2015), "Occupational Outlook Handbook" http://www.bls.gov/ooh/office-and-administrative-support/tellers.htm

[3] E. Florian (2004), "The Money Machines The humble ATM revolutionized the way we deal with money and turned global commerce into a 24/7 affair. You can thank a Texan named Don Wetzel--and the blizzard of 1978" http://archive.fortune.com/magazines/fortune/fortune_archive/2004/07/26/377172/index.htm

[4] Chaia I, Goland T, Schiff R (2010) "Counting the World's Unbanked" http://www.mckinsey.com/industries/financial-services/our-insights/counting-the-worlds-unbanked

[5] IFC Advisory Services (2011) "Access To Credit Among Micro, Small, And Medium Enterprises" http://www.ifc.org/wps/wcm/connect/1f2c968041689903950bb79e78015671/AccessCreditMSME-Brochure-Final.pdf?MOD=AJPERES

[6] H. Broeders and S. Khanna (2015), "Strategic choices for banks in the digital age", McKinsey & Company

[7] G. Prisco (2015) " Enigma, MIT Media Lab's Blockchain-based Encrypted Data Marketplace, to Launch Beta" https://bitcoinmagazine.com/articles/enigma-mit-media-lab-s-blockchain-based-encrypted-data-marketplace-to-launch-beta-1450810499

[8] For example, in Asia the number of potential digital-banking consumers could be as high as 1.7 billion by 2020, see J. Chen, V. HV, K. Lam (2015), "How to prepare for Asia's digital-banking boom", McKinsey & Company

9 D. Shrier, J. Larossi, D. Sharma and A. Pentland (2016) "Blockchain & Transactions, Markets and Marketplaces" http://resources.getsmarter.ac/other/the-mit-report-on-blockchain-part-2/

10 D. Shrier, G. Canale and A. Pentland (2016) "Mobile Money & Payments: Technology Trends" http://resources.getsmarter.ac/other/mobile-money-payments-technology-trends-an-mit-white-paper/

[11] S. Das (2016) "Japanese Banking Giant Reveals Plans for a Digital Currency" https://www.cryptocoinsnews.com/japanese-banking-giant-reveals-plans-for-a-digital-currency/

[12] It is necessary to provide customers with proper privacy safeguards.

[13] It is possible that both tech premium and financial discount are temporary in nature.

CHAPTER 7: POLICY & FINTECH

[1] Goodenough, O. R. (2015), "Legal Technology 3.0," Huffington Post, February 4, 2015, available at http://www.huffingtonpost.com/oliver-r-goodenough/legal-technology-30_b_6603658.html?utm_hp_ref=tw

[2] For convenience, we refer to distributed cryptographic ledgers generically as "blockchain" or "blockchain technology," even though certain variants, such as R3/Corda, don't use blocks.

[3] Some discussions of "regulation" limit that term to the more narrow class of rules made by governmental agencies such as the Environmental Protection Agency or Securities Exchange Commission. In this book, we use the term in the broader context of governmentally originated rules as described in the text.

[4] Dudley, S. E. and Brito, J. (2012), Regulation: A Primer, https://regulatorystudies.columbian.gwu.edu/sites/regulatorystudies.columbian.gwu.edu/files/downloads/RegulatoryPrimer_DudleyBrito.pdf .

[5] Office of Management and Budget (2003), "Circular A-4," https://www.whitehouse.gov/omb/circulars_a004_a-4/

[96] Leigh Bureau, (2012), "Paul Romer," Speaker Biography, http://web.archive.org/web/20120606014844/http://www.leighbureau.com/speakers/promer/romer.pdf.

[7] Greenberg, A. (2015), "Silk Road Creator Ross Ulbricht Sentenced to Life in Prison," Wired, 29 May 2015, https://www.wired.com/2015/05/silk-road-creator-ross-ulbricht-sentenced-life-prison/.

[8] Magaziner, I. (1999), "Creating a Framework for Global Electronic Commerce," Future Insight, The Progress and Freedom Foundation, 6(1), July, http://www.pff.org/issues-pubs/futureinsights/fi6.1globaleconomiccommerce.html.

[9] Drobac, J. A. and Goodenough, O. R. (2015) "Exposing the Myth of Consent," Indiana Health Law Review, http://ssrn.com/abstract=2559341

[10] Vermont General Assembly (2016), "An act relating to miscellaneous economic development provisions," Bill as passed by the House and Senate, H.868, http://legislature.vermont.gov/assets/Documents/2016/Docs/BILLS/H-0868/H-0868%20As%20Passed%20by%20Both%20House%20and%20Senate%20Official.pdf.

[11] Hamilton A (2016) "Japan Central Bank official: Keep an eye on Bitcoin and blockchain" IBS Intelligence https://ibsintelligence.com/ibs-journal/ibs-news/japan-central-bank-official-keep-an-eye-on-bitcoin-and-blockchain/

[12] Gomex, E. (2016) "Barbados Wants To Become The Caribbean FinTech Capital" TheMerkle.com http://themerkle.com/barbados-wants-to-become-the-caribbean-fintech-capital/

[13] Meyer, Eugene, Jr. (1922), "Financing Agriculture," Address before the State Bank Division

of the American Bankers Association, New York, October 2, 1922, https://archive.org/download/financingagricu00meye/financingagricu00meye.pdf.

[14] Broadbent, B. (2016), "Central banks and digital currencies," Speech at the London School of Economics, 2 March 2016, Bank of England, http://www.bankofengland.co.uk/publications/Pages/speeches/2016/886.aspx.

[15] Bank for International Settlements (2015), "Digital currencies," November, http://www.bis.org/cpmi/publ/d137.pdf.

[16] Office of Information and Regulatory Affairs (2016), "Regulatory Impact Analysis: A Primer," https://www.whitehouse.gov/sites/default/files/omb/inforeg/regpol/circular-a-4_regulatory-impact-analysis-a-primer.pdf .

[17] Zittrain, J. (2008), The Future of the Internet and How to Stop It, Yale University Press.

[18] Goodenough, O. (2015), "Generativity: Making Law a More Open Institutional 'Ecosystem' for Productive Innovation", Vermont Law School Paper No. 4-15, http://papers.ssrn.com/sol3/papers.cfm?abstract_id=2589263.

[19] Nasdaq (2016) "Building on the Blockchain: Nasdaq's vision of Innovation" http://business.nasdaq.com/Docs//Blockchain%20Report%20March%202016_tcm5044-26461.pdf

[20] Kaplow, L. (1992), "Rules Versus Standards: An Economic Analysis", Duke Law Journal 42:557-629, http://scholarship.law.duke.edu/dlj/vol42/iss3/2

[21] Lessig, L. (2005), Codev2, http://codev2.cc/download+remix/Lessig-Codev2.pdf.

[22] Vigna, P (2014) "5 Things About Mt. Gox's Crisis" Wall St. Journal Blog, http://blogs.wsj.com/briefly/2014/02/25/5-things-about-mt-goxs-crisis/

[23] Delaware Office of the Governor (2016), "Governor Markell Launches Delaware Blockchain Initiative," PR Newswire, http://www.prnewswire.com/news-releases/governor-markell-launches-delaware-blockchain-initiative-300260672.html

[24] Uniform Law Commission (1999), "Uniform Electronic Transactions Act (1999)," National Conference of Commissioners on Uniform State Laws, http://www.uniformlaws.org/Act.aspx?title=Electronic%20Transactions%20Act.

[25] Vermont General Assembly (2010), "Vermont Business Corporations: Incorporation: Bylaws," Vermont Statutes Online, 11(A)(2)(06), http://legislature.vermont.gov/statutes/section/11A/002/00002.06.

[26] Wolinsky, A. (1995), "Competition in Markets for Credence Goods," Journal of Institutional Theoretical Economics 151:117–31.

[27] Federal Deposit Insurance Corporation (FDIC) (2005), "Role of the Transfer Agent," Section 11 in: Trust Examination Manual, https://www.fdic.gov/regulations/examinations/trustmanual/section_11/rta_manualroleoftransferagent.html.

[28] Popper, N. (2012) "Knight Capital Says Trading Glitch Cost It $440 Million" The New York Times http://dealbook.nytimes.com/2012/08/02/knight-capital-says-trading-mishap-cost-

it-440-million/?_r=0

[29] Mary-Ann Russon (2016) "The curious tale of Ethereum: How a hacker stole $53m in digital currency and could legally keep it," International Business Times, http://www.ibtimes.co.uk/curious-tale-ethereum-how-hacker-stole-53m-digital-currency-could-legally-keep-it-1566524

[30] Andrew Quentson (2016) "Ethereum Devs Hack the Hacker, Price Skyrockets," Crypto Coins News https://www.cryptocoinsnews.com/ethereum-devs-hack-the-hacker-price-skyrockets/

[31] "How to clean TRACE Data" (2016) Copenhagen Business School Department of Finance http://sf.cbs.dk/jdnielsen/how_to_clean_trace_data

[32] Global Legal Entity Identifier Foundation (2016), "Annual Report 2015," https://www.gleif.org/content/1-about/5-governance/10-annual-report/2016-05-03_gleif_2015_annual_report_final.pdf.

[33] D. Atkins, W. Stallings, P. Zimmerman, PGP Message Exchange Formats, IETF RFC1991, August 1996, Internet Engineering Task Force.

[34] D. L. Chaum, "Untraceable electronic mail, return addresses, and digital pseudonyms," Communications of the ACM, vol. 24, no. 2, pp. 84–88, February 1981.

[35] ABC4Trust, Attribute-based Credentials for Trust, https://abc4trust.eu

[36] G. Zyskind, O. Nathan and A. Pentland, "Enigma: Decentralized Computation Platform with Guaranteed Privacy", available at http://enigma.mit.edu/enigma_full.pdf

[37] FICAM, U.S. Federal Identity, Credential and Access Management (FICAM) Program, http://info.idmanagement.gov

[38] OIX, OpenID Exchange, http://openidentityexchange.org

[39] SAFE-BioPharma Association, Trust Framework Provider Services, http://www.safe-biopharma.org/SAFE_Trust_Framework.htm

[40] See, e.g., Ali, R (2014), "Innovations in payment technologies and the emergence of digital currencies," Bank of England Quarterly Bulletin, http://www.bankofengland.co.uk/publications/Documents/quarterlybulletin/2014/qb14q3digitalcurrenciesbitcoin1.pdf

[41] ISDA (2014) "Major Banks Agree to Sign ISDA Resolution Stay Protocol" http://www2.isda.org/news/major-banks-agree-to-sign-isda-resolution-stay-protocol

Contributor Biographies

David Shrier is Managing Director of MIT Connection Science and leads creation and launch of other new initiatives for the Massachusetts Institute of Technology. He is also on the advisory board of WorldQuant University, which offers a totally free, online, accredited master's degree in analytics. David recently advised the European Commission on commercializing innovation with a focus on digital technology, and advises private and public companies on corporate innovation. David specializes in building new revenue on established platforms, having developed $8.5 billion of growth opportunities with companies including GE/NBC Universal, Dun & Bradstreet, Wolters Kluwer, Disney, Ernst & Young, AOL Verizon, and Starwood Hotels & Resorts, as well as leading private equity and VC funds. He has also started and/or led a number of private equity and venture capital-backed companies as CEO, CFO or COO. David created a revolutionary online fintech startup learning experience for MIT called "Fintech Innovation: Future Commerce", that is deployed into 70 countries, and also teaches courses and workshops for MIT such as "Data Academy", "Inspiring Change: Strategic Narrative for Startup Success", "Big Data and Social Analytics", and "Future Health". David Shrier was granted an Sc.B. from Brown University in Biology and Theatre.

Professor Alex "Sandy" Pentland holds a triple appointment at the Massachusetts Institute of Technology in the Media Lab (SA+P), School of Engineering and School of Management. He also directs MIT's Connect Science initiative, the Human Dynamics Laboratory and the MIT Media Lab Entrepreneurship Program, and has been a member of the Advisory Boards for Google, Nissan, Telefonica, Tencent, and a variety of start-up firms. For several years he co-led the World Economic Forum Big Data and Personal Data initiatives. He has pioneered the fields of wearable computing and computational social science, generating several successful startups and technology spinoffs. Sandy was recently named by the Secretary-General of the United Nations to the Independent Expert Advisory Group on the Data Revolution for Sustainable Development. His article, "The New Science of Building Great Teams", won paper of the year in 2012 from Harvard Business Review. Sandy has previously helped create and direct MIT's Media Laboratory, the Media Lab Asia laboratories at the Indian Institutes of Technology, and Strong Hospital's Center for Future Health. He recently led a task force on big data & healthcare for the World Innovation Summit in Healthcare, held in Doha, Qatar. In 2012 Forbes named Sandy one of the "seven most powerful data scientists in the world", along with the founders of Google and the CTO of the United States, and in 2013 he won the McKinsey Award from Harvard Business Review. Prof. Pentland's books include Honest Signals and Social Physics. He was named to the National Academy of Engineering in 2014. Sandy holds a BGS from the University of Michigan and a Ph.D. from MIT.

Oliver Goodenough is an authority on several emerging areas of law. He has pioneered the application of technology to legal processes, particularly in the field of contracts and business organizations. His goal is to create "digital institutions" within which reliable economic life can take place. In Vermont, he has been a participant in the legislatively-mandated Blockchain study committee and is a co-author of recent pioneering legislation that give Blockchain technology legal recognition. At the national level, he is collaborating with the Office of Financial Research at the Department of the Treasury to explore the possibility of automating financial instruments. Professor Goodenough's other fields of research include entertainment law and applications of neuroscience and behavioral biology to legal questions. He is currently a Professor of Law and the Director of the Center for Legal Innovation at Vermont Law

School, Affiliated Faculty at Stanford's CodeX Center for Legal Informatics, a Research Fellow of the Gruter Institute for Law and Behavioral Research, a Lecturer at the University of Vermont's School of Business Administration, and an Adjunct Professor at Dartmouth's Thayer School of Engineering. He has previously been a Faculty Fellow at Harvard's Berkman Center for Internet & Society and a Visiting Research Fellow at the Cambridge University Department of Zoology.

Thomas Hardjono is the CTO of MIT Connection Science and Engineering. He leads technical projects and initiatives around identity, security and data privacy, and engages industry partners and sponsors on these fronts. Thomas is also the technical director for the Internet Trust Consortium under MIT Connection Science that implements open source software based on cutting edge research at MIT. The consortium embodies the MIT philosophy of giving back to the community. Over the years he has published three books and over sixty technical papers in journals and at conferences. He holds 19 patents in the areas of security and cryptography. Thomas has a BSc degree in Computer Science with Honors from the University of Sydney, and PhD degree in Computer Science from the University of New South Wales in Australia.

Alexander Lipton is an MIT Connection Science Fellow. He was mostly recently a Managing Director, Quantitative Solutions Executive at Bank of America. Prior to that, he was a Managing Director, Co-head of the Global Quantitative Group at Bank of America Merrill Lynch. He also held senior managerial positions at several sell and buy side firms. Currently, Alexander is an Adjunct Professor of Mathematics at NYU. Previously, he was a Visiting Professor of Quantitative Finance and Advisory Board member at the Oxford-Man Institute, University of Oxford. Earlier, he was a Visiting Professor of Mathematics at Imperial College London. Before switching to finance, Alex was a Full Professor of Mathematics at the University of Illinois and a Consultant at Los Alamos National Laboratory. He is the first recipient of the prestigious Quant of the Year award.

Deven Sharma, an MIT Connection Science Fellow, served as President of Standard & Poor's, Head of Global Strategy and M&A at The McGraw-Hill Companies and partner at Booz Allen Hamilton. He served as Chairman of Crisil, an Indian public company, and member of 800-Flowers board. Deven is the founder of InfleXon, a firm focused on strategic transformation through disruptions in information, technology and geo political markets, as well as in risk and regulatory governance. He also invests and advises growth and start up companies in technology and analytic enabled services. Deven holds a PhD in Operations Management from The Ohio State University, MS in Industrial Engineering from University of Wisconsin, and BS from Birla Institute of Technology.

Dhaval Adjodah is a PhD student at the MIT Media Lab in the Human Dynamics group. He is interested in the intersection of mathematical modeling of human interaction, socio-economic development and governance. Previously, he worked in Big Data consulting and finance, and completed a Bachelors in Physics and and a Masters in Policy, both from MIT.

Jackie Larossi is a senior manger with the new ventures team at BBVA's innovation office in San Francisco. She received her MBA from MIT Sloan and previously worked for Morgan Stanley and Capgemini.

German Canale Segovia is co-founder of Domo Capital, a search fund based in Mexico. He received his MBA from MIT Sloan and previously was a successful entrepreneur (CRO of Credex), university instructor (Universidad Panamericana) and private equity / VC professional (Bain; Angel Ventures).

Weige Wu is an Associate at McKinsey & Co. in the New York office. She grew up in Singapore and previously worked in London for McKinsey, and holds a MBA in Finance and Sustainability from MIT Sloan and a BA in Philosophy, Politics, and Economics from the University of Oxford.

67868595R00136

Made in the USA
Lexington, KY
24 September 2017